CHRIST AND CHRISTIANITY

Studies in the Formation of Christology

Reginald H. Fuller

Compiled, Edited, and with an Introduction
by Robert Kahl

Trinity Press International   Valley Forge, Pennsylvania

First Edition 1994

Trinity Press International
P.O. Box 851
Valley Forge, PA 19482-0851

Cover design by Gene Harris

Library of Congress Cataloging-in-Publication Data

Fuller, Reginald Horace.
    Christ and Christianity : studies in the formation of Christology
/ Reginald H. Fuller : compiled, edited, and with an introduction by
Robert Kahl. — 1st ed.
      p.   cm.
    Includes bibliographical references and index.
    ISBN 1-56338-076-5 :
    1. Jesus Christ—History of doctrines—Early church, ca. 30–600.
2. Jesus Christ—Person and offices. 3. Bible. N.T. Gospels—
Criticism, interpretation, etc. 4. Anglican Communion—Doctrines.
I. Kahl, Robert. II. Title.
BT198.F88   1994
232—dc20
                                  94-15803
                                      CIP

Printed in the United States of America.

94 95 96 97 98   6 5 4 3 2 1

Grateful acknowledgment is made to the following for permission to reprint previously published material:

Cambridge University Press for "Sir Edwyn Hoskyns and the Contemporary Relevance of 'Biblical Theology,'" *New Testament Studies* 30 (1984): 321–44.

Akademie Verlag, Berlin, for "The Clue to Jesus' Self-understanding," *Studia Evangelica* 3 (1964): 58–66, Texte und Untersuchungen 88; and "New Testament Trajectories and Biblical Authority," *Studia Evangelica* 7 (1982): 189–99, Texte und Untersuchungen 126.

Christian Theological Seminary for "The Church Under the Lordship of Jesus Christ," *Encounter* 20 (1959): 446–50.

North Park College for "The Resurrection of Jesus Christ," *Biblical Research* 4 (1960): 8–24.

The *Anglican Theological Review* for "The Incarnation in Historical Perspective," in *Theology and Culture: Essays in Honor of Albert T. Mollegen and Clifford L. Stanley,* ed. W. Taylor Stephenson, Anglican Theological Review Supplementary Series 7 (1976): 57–66.

The University of Dayton for "New Testament Roots to the *Theotokos,*" *Marian Studies* 29 (1978): 49–64.

Union Theological Seminary, Richmond, for "Jesus Christ as Savior in the New Testament," *Interpretation* 35 (1981): 145–56.

Vandenhoeck & Ruprecht, Göttingen, for "Early Catholicism: An Anglican Reaction to a German Debate," in *In Die Mitte des Neuen Testaments: Einheit und Vielfalt Neutestamentlicher Theologie; Festschrift für Eduard Schweizer on His 70th Birthday,* ed. Ulrich Luz and Hans Weder (1983): 34–41.

Luther Northwestern Seminary for "Preexistence Christology: Can We Dispense with It?" *Word and World* 2 (1982): 29–33.

CONTENTS

PART SIX
The Post-Easter Church

ACKNOWLEDGMENTS

I want to thank the following people without whose generous help *Christ and Christianity* would not have been possible: Gerald P. Burke, Administrative Assistant, Church of the Advent, Cape May, New Jersey, who typed the précis of the essays contained in this collection as well as the first draft of the introduction, and kept track of the letters of consent from the various publishers of Reginald Fuller's essays; and Edith S. (Mrs. Harry D.) Lemmon, Directress of the Altar Guild and licensed Layreader, Chalicebearer, and Eucharistic Minister of the Church of the Advent, who proofread the final draft of the introduction and made many helpful comments leading to the improvements of its style, grammar, and understandability.

I would also like to thank the staff of the Speer Memorial Library, Princeton Theological Seminary, for their assistance and the use of their facilities.

With deep filial affection and gratitude, and with Reginald Fuller's blessing, I dedicate *Christ and Christianity* to the loving memory of my late parents, Anna Luella (Brown) and Robert Mathew Kahl.

ROBERT KAHL

ABBREVIATIONS

AB	Anchor Bible
ANTJ	Arbeiten zum Neuen Testament und Judentum
ATR	*Anglican Theological Review*
BEvT	Beiträge zur evangelischen Theologie
BibRes	*Biblical Research*
BZNW	Beihefte zur Zeitschrift für die neutestamentliche Wissenschaft
CBQ	*Catholic Biblical Quarterly*
EvT	*Evangelische Theologie*
FRLANT	Forschungen zur Religion und Literatur des Alten und Neuen Testaments
HNTC	Harper's New Testament Commentaries
HTR	*Harvard Theological Review*
JBL	*Journal of Biblical Literature*
JR	*Journal of Religion*
JTC	*Journal for Theology and the Church*
JTS	*Journal of Theological Studies*
KD	*Kerygma und Dogma*
LTK	*Lexicon für Theologie und Kirche*
NCB	New Century Bible
NTD	Das Neue Testament Deutsch
NTL	New Testament Library
NTS	*New Testament Studies*
RB	*Revue biblique*

RGG	*Religion in Geschichte und Gegenwart*
SBL	Society of Biblical Literature
SBT	Studies in Biblical Theology
SNT	Studien zum Neuen Testament
SNTS	Society for New Testament Studies
SNTSMS	Society for New Testament Studies Monograph Series
TDNT	*Theological Dictionary of the New Testament*
TF	*Theologische Forschung*
TWNT	*Theologisches Wörterbuch zur Neuen Testament*
TZ	*Theologische Zeitschrift*
ZNW	*Zeitschrift für die neutestamentliche Wissenschaft*
ZTK	*Zeitschrift für Theologie und Kirche*

INTRODUCTION

Late on a Saturday evening in December of 1975, I was about to take the Right Reverend Stephen C. Neill from my apartment to his motel room. I was then serving as curate at Trinity Church, Moorestown, New Jersey, and Neill was scheduled to preach there the next day. On our way to the stairs, Neill saw a copy of Reginald Fuller's *The Formation of the Resurrection Narratives* lying on my kitchen table. Even though Neill knew that Fuller had been my New Testament professor when I was a graduate student at Union Theological Seminary, New York, that did not prevent him from saying, "You know, about the only things Reginald and I can agree upon are the grace of our Lord Jesus Christ, the love of God, and the fellowship of Cambridge University. Would you mind terribly if I were to borrow this book for the evening? I want to see what Reginald is believing these days, if anything at all. But that's not quite fair, since Reginald is about the only person I know who can punch a passage of scripture black and blue and still retain a child-like faith in the goodness and love of God."

Without realizing it, Neill had summarized, admittedly in a negative way, what Fuller had always practiced throughout his many years as priest and scholar. Whereas Neill implied that Fuller believed in spite of the historical-critical method, the latter has consistently maintained that not only his faith, but faith itself has been and can be strengthened because of that method.

In 1989, Fuller discussed with me the possibility of editing some of his christological essays into book form. Schillebeeckx's *Jesus* had been translated from the Dutch into English, and his *Grechtigheid en liefde: Genade en bevrijding* was about to appear in translation as *Christ*. Even though Fuller was greatly impressed that a systematic theologian should master the historical-critical method, and although he found the chapters on the historical Jesus superb in every way, he was somewhat disappointed in Schillebeeckx's Bultmannian treatment of the resurrection.

Fuller believed, nevertheless, that Schillebeeckx had attempted something that present-day biblical scholars had been overlooking—the theological exposition of the text. Before the time that *Jesus* had appeared in English and ten years before the English-language edition of *Christ,* Fuller had written in *St. Luke's Journal of Theology* of the need for systematic theologians to be better critics and for critics to become more astute systematic theologians; and he reiterated this concern in 1984 in *Anglicanism and the Bible.*

> In 1980 the present writer wrote of a need for a moratorium on historical-critical discussion as far as the New Testament is concerned. A little injudiciously, perhaps, he spoke of the "bankruptcy" of the historical-critical method. What he had in mind was the ever more minute dissecting of the text that forms the staple content of Ph.D. theses today. Instead he called for a shift of emphasis to the theological exegesis of the biblical text, and for a renewed commitment on the part of the biblical scholars to seeing their task as a service to the church. He proposed "that critical scholars . . . should impose upon themselves the self-denying ordinance of a moratorium of historical-critical analysis of the Gospels and the Pauline homologoumena and concentrate upon their theological exegesis." This was not a call for a fundamentalist abandonment of the historical-critical method. That method has yielded indispensable tools for the theological exegesis that is needed. But it does mean that historical criticism supplies us only with the tools and concerns itself only with the prolegomena to our real task which is the theological-critical interpretation of the text.[1]

Fuller best stated his understanding of the historical-critical method and the effect it had on him as priest and Christian in October and November 1991 when he delivered a series of lectures on the Fourth Gospel at Nashotah House, a seminary of the

Episcopal Church near Milwaukee. At the beginning of these four addresses, which were based in part on J. A. T. Robinson's posthumously published Bampton Lectures, *The Priority of John,* and on C. H. Dodd's *The Interpretation of the Fourth Gospel,* Fuller drew on ironic contrast between Robinson and himself. The more Robinson used the historical-critical method, the more traditional, conservative, the more "pre-Germanic"—that is, "English"—his conclusions regarding the origin and development of the New Testament became, as was best demonstrated in his *Redating the New Testament.* In other words, Robinson's use of "Germanic" methods, which suggested that the Fourth Gospel was the product of protracted development, enabled him to "take up the cause" of the "pre-Germanic," or "English," school, which allowed for almost no evolution in the composition of the Fourth Gospel. At the same time, however, his use of the historical-traditional method made him all the more convinced of the rightness of German existential theology, which was the basis for *Honest to God.* Biblical criticism had made him biblically conservative and theologically liberal.

Fuller, on the other hand, said that although the historical-critical method had led him to critical "Germanic" conclusions with regard to the origins and development of the New Testament, theologically he remained as he had always been—a pre-Tractarian High Church Anglican. The critical process had made him biblically critical and theologically orthodox.

In his most recent book, *He That Cometh,* Fuller said that the "reality" of God in Christ was manifested and perceived earlier than was previously supposed. In so doing he took to task one of the conclusions of such contemporary biblical scholars as Raymond Brown (as seen in *The Birth of the Messiah*). It was Brown's belief that the "moving back," or the retrojection, of a decisive christological moment from the resurrection to the baptism and from there to the nativity, and thence to preexistence, was a late development in the evolution of the New Testament. His conclusions continued to leave the Bultmannian door open to the possibility that such doctrines contingent to preexistence and Nicea's "three-tiered Christology" (the virginal conception, virgin birth, and bodily resurrection) belonged more to the realm of metaphor and myth than to the arena of history—that something could be *Geschichte* (of significant history) without first being *Historie* (mere history).

Systematic Christology, of course, reflects upon and studies the divinity and humanity of Christ and how each is present in one person. Such a systematic understanding has been made possible because a first-century, Aramaic-speaking Jewish prophet, Jesus of Nazareth, made an eschatological claim that through his words, his works, and his death, God was acting eschatologically, at last fulfilling all the promises that had been made to Israel. Moreover, God had vindicated this prophet's claim in raising him from the dead and proclaiming him to the church through the Holy Spirit to be both Lord and Christ.

The post-Easter church responded to the Christ event with a kerygma, a proclamation: Good Friday was the redemptive act of God. The early writers of the New Testament—first-, second-, and perhaps even third-generation Christians—made assessments largely on a functional nature: What exactly was it that God had accomplished in Jesus, now Lord and Christ? As the church encountered Hellenistic Jews and Gentiles, the questions became increasingly ontological in nature: Who is this Christ?

Subapostolic, ontological Christology came into full flower during the conciliar era. However, this sort of christological investigation is not entirely absent from the New Testament. The seeds of conciliar Christology can in fact be found in such post-Easter titles as Wisdom, Logos, and in the ontological reinterpretation of the titles "Christ," "Son of God," "Lord," the pre-Pauline christological hymns and statements, the nativities according to Matthew and Luke, the deutero-Pauline letters of Ephesians, and Colossians, the anti-*theios anēr* sayings of the Gospel according to Mark, and the compositional (or discourse) stage of the Fourth Gospel, which were "imposed" on the sayings of the historical Jesus because of the Easter event wherein the post-Easter church had come to perceive that the Proclaimer had become the Proclaimed.[2]

The tools for such christological reflection in the New Testament were the sayings of the historical Jesus and the earliest kerygma, Jesus as he was proclaimed by his disciples during the era of oral transmission and the formation of the passion and resurrection narratives. For the type of ontological reflection we find after the close of the first century C.E. to the full-blown Christology we trace from Nicea to Chalcedon, as well as all christological inquiries subsequent to 451 C.E., we can add the witness of the entire New Testament (as well as apocryphal material). Finally, the contemporary situation has been and always will be a constant factor (but never the deciding factor) in the shape and content of all christological statements.

Today, in the postcritical era, when we speak of the preaching or message of Jesus, it has become both customary and necessary to distinguish between the subjective and objective genitive; that is, between the words of the earthly Jesus and the church's preaching about Jesus. Prior to the early fifties, when Rudolf Bultmann was generally acknowledged to be the most influential figure in New Testament studies and the one whose existential interpretation had become the criterion for New Testament exegesis for over a generation, it was taken for granted that the study of Jesus of Nazareth began with the kerygma of the earliest Christian communities and that the message *of* Jesus could not be received—only the message *about* Jesus. It was Bultmann's contention that the New Testament could take us back to the resurrection faith of the earliest disciples and no further; that "all that historical criticism can establish is the fact that the first disciples came to believe in the resurrection."[3] The New Testament, following Bultmann's logic, does not present us with the history of a person who was born during the time of Caesar Augustus and crucified under Pontius Pilate; rather, it challenges us to make existential decisions of potentially historic proportions. According to Bultmann, the great question for the Christ is not "Who is Jesus?" but "Who is Jesus for me?"

In October 1953 Ernst Käsemann, one of Bultmann's students, delivered a paper entitled "The Problem of the Historical Jesus." After recognizing the validity and importance of his mentor's contributions to New Testament study, he proceeded to challenge an almost unquestioned tenet of nearly four decades of German scholarship: that the quest for the historical Jesus was impossible and, even if it were possible, it was irrelevant and distracting. In contrast, Käsemann argued that not only can something be known about the historical Jesus, but exegesis itself must be involved in making this "something" known if we do not want ultimately to find ourselves committed to a mythological Lord.[4] This lecture, it can be fairly said, marked the beginning of the post-Bultmannian era in Germany.

Another of Bultmann's students, Günther Bornkamm, followed suit with the publication of *Jesus von Nazareth* (1956). Bornkamm held that although it is practically impossible to write a biography of Jesus, the very critical methods that scholars of another generation had used to separate faith from history can be used to give "a historical presentation of Christ and his message."

One of the first challenges to Bultmann's existential claims, however, came from a British scholar, Reginald H. Fuller, who from 1955 to 1985 held chairs in New Testament studies at Seabury-Western Theological Seminary in Evanston, Illinois, Union Theological Seminary in New York City, and Virginia Theological Seminary in Alexandria, Virginia.

Fuller has not always written exclusively from an anti-Bultmannian perspective, but from the vantage point of the British (especially the Cambridge) tradition of Westcott, Hort, and Lightfoot, and of his beloved mentor Sir Edwyn Clement Hoskyns. For these eminent scholars, the quest for the historical Jesus had been relatively long, uninterrupted, and untroubled.[5]

In 1951, two years before the epochal Käsemann lecture and five years before *Jesus von Nazareth,* Fuller, then Professor of Theology and Hebrew (though in practice he taught only New Testament) at David's College in Lampeter, Wales, delivered a series of lectures on the historical Jesus that were published in 1954 as a monograph entitled *The Mission and Achievement of Jesus.* As the Käsemann lecture, *Mission* (by way of being a response to Bultmann's thirty-page treatment of Jesus in the first volume of his *Theology of the New Testament*) was an attempt to establish a continuity between the historical Jesus and the post-Easter church. What was significant about *Mission* was that it was written in complete ignorance of the "new quest" that was just beginning in

Germany. (In remarks to me, Fuller made Jesus' messianic consciousness more explicit than had the "new questers"; he has since modified his views.[6]) Seven years later, in 1961, he was awarded a fellowship by the American Association of Theological Schools that took him to Germany for a meeting where he met Günther Bornkamm and his assistant, Ferdinand Hahn, who allowed Fuller to read his doctoral dissertation *Christologische Hoheitstitel* and to avail himself of his bibliography. The result of the fellowship and of Fuller's association with Bornkamm and Hahn was his *chef d'oeuvre, The Foundations of New Testament Christology.*

Here Fuller goes beyond the work of the German-speaking, post-Bultmannian scholars by not only tracing the continuity between the eschatological message of the historical Jesus and the christological kerygma of the postresurrection church, but also in "unearthing" a skeleton that holds the New Testament together and sets the boundaries for christological inquiries subsequent to the New Testament—the least and the most the church can claim about the work and person, the humanity and divinity of Jesus of Nazareth.

Fuller begins *Foundations* with a discussion of the three cultures that helped shape New Testament Christology: Palestinian Judaism, Hellenistic Judaism, and the worldview of the Greek-speaking Gentile. These environments largely provided the vocabulary that enabled the evangelists and other writers of the first century C.E. to respond to, proclaim, and interpret to their respective communities the message of the historical Jesus and the significance of his cross and resurrection as proclaimed by the post-Easter church.

After a careful analysis of Palestinian Judaism, Hellenistic Judaism, and the religions of the Hellenistic Gentile world, Fuller proceeds to a thoroughgoing discussion of three christological patterns in the New Testament: earliest Palestinian, Hellenistic Jewish, and the Gentile mission. The bases of these emerging Christologies were the ever-changing needs of the church from the Easter event until the time that the body faithful had accepted the fact that the *parousia* had been indefinitely postponed, a period of some sixty years.

The result of the church's contact with the shifting needs of three very different cultures was a three-tiered Christology: Christ preached, believed, and worshiped as the expected Messiah; the exalted Lord and Giver of the Spirit; and the preexistent Word of God.

The format of *Christ and Christianity* roughly follows that of *Foundations*. However, whereas *Foundations* does not discuss in depth the particular Christologies of, say, Paul, Mark, Luke, John, and the author of the letter to the Hebrews, *Christ and Christianity* does. Fuller's earlier book provides us with a backbone, a set of ribs, two tibias, and two femurs. The purpose of the present book is to examine the work of some of the writers of the New Testament and to add, as it were, the vital organs.

Christ and Christianity hopes to accomplish four things: (1) to stimulate more study of the continuity between the message of Jesus and the message about Jesus—the "new" quest for the historical Jesus; (2) to provide grist for the theologian's and the exegete's mill, encouraging the former to become a better biblical scholar and the latter a more formidable theologian and, at the same time, to remind them of the irony of the theological enterprise (that although God's revelation in Christ was complete, the various methods the theologian and exegete have at their disposal—language, logic, intuition—are always imprecise and incomplete); (3) to present a survey of the work of one of this century's most important New Testament scholars; and (4) to reintroduce and refamiliarize serious students of scripture with a method that at best can be called uniquely Anglican—a scholarly and prayerful listening to the voices of scripture, tradition, and reason.[7]

Many of the essays in this volume were, of course, written before we had become aware of and sensitive to our use of sexist or noninclusive language in theological literature. To revise passages that now seem too masculine, however, even those relating to the Deity, would have been formidable and would have risked changing the author's meaning. For the most part, then, the essays have been allowed to stand in their original form, and the reader's understanding of this matter is greatly appreciated.

Finally, this collection of Reginald Fuller's principal christological essays is being offered to the church as encouragement, and as a guide for pondering the message of Jesus and presenting the message about Jesus to a world about to enter a new millennium.

Notes

1. Frederick H. Borsch, ed., *Anglicanism and the Bible* (Wilton, Conn.: Morehouse Publishing, 1986), 167–68.

2. Reginald H. Fuller and Pheme Perkins, *Who Is This Christ? Gospel Christology and Contemporary Faith* (Philadelphia: Fortress Press, 1983), 41.

3. James M. Robinson, *A New Quest for the Historical Jesus* (Philadelphia: Fortress Press, 1983), 13.

4. Günther Bornkamm, *Jesus of Nazareth* (New York: Harper & Row, 1975), 14.

5. Robinson, *New Quest,* 9.

6. Reginald H. Fuller, *The Foundations of New Testament Christology* (New York: Charles Scribner's Sons, 1965), 11.

7. In a recent conversation, Fuller repeated what a German biblical scholar had once said to him: "Everytime you Anglicans are about to do something important, the bell rings and off you go to Evensong." In a somewhat unflattering way, this critic had expressed the essence of the Anglican method: a careful, judicious weighing of scripture, tradition, and reason in the light of the liturgy, theology, and both systematic and ascetic principles of the *Book of Common Prayer.* Anglicans at their best have always tried to maintain the synergistic relationship between worship and dogma, doxology and investigation.

From Exegesis to Christology

1

SIR EDWYN HOSKYNS AND THE CONTEMPORARY RELEVANCE OF "BIBLICAL THEOLOGY"

Biblical Theology: A Detour?

In the early 1950s a cartoon appeared in Punch depicting a British motorist able at last to resume touring the continent after World War II. The first scene shows a straight, tree-lined chaussée, with the driver saying to his passenger, "Now for these lovely straight French roads." In the next scene they quickly come to a barrier with the warning "Déviation 19 kilomètres."

In recent years it has been fashionable to denigrate what is often, though inaccurately,[1] referred to as "the biblical theology movement" (of which Sir Edwyn Hoskyns was one of the pioneers) as just such a *déviation*. In an essay published under the title "Salvation: Traditions and Reappraisals,"[2] the late Geoffrey Lampe has told us that when he went to Queen's College under the Rev. J. O. Cobham in 1936, Queen's was dominated by "Hoskyns . . . and Barthian neo-orthodoxy" fostered by its relation to the Evangelisches Stift in Tübingen. "The questions raised by the Liberal Protestantism of the earlier years of the century apparently seemed to have been the wrong questions to ask." But now, continued Lampe, "after forty years the picture is dramatically different." The questions raised by the older liberal Protestantism have returned in a much more urgent form. We have now resumed the proper task of reconciling traditional theology with modern thought.

Nor is Lampe alone in this view of biblical theology as a *détour*. The turning point seems to have come in 1961 with the important essay by the American scholar J. Langdon Gilkey entitled "Cosmology, Ontology, and the Travail of Biblical Language."[3] Gilkey argues that biblical theology (he had in mind the work of the OT theologians G. E. Wright and B. Anderson) was unsatisfactory because it was "half liberal and half orthodox." Using the historical-critical method, it reduced the basic historically verifiable events of the Bible to a bare minimum (the exodus event was simply an east wind blowing over the Red Sea, the Easter event merely a few subjective visions); yet as orthodox theologians these scholars insisted on speaking of such events as "mighty acts of God." Most of the alleged mighty acts of God recorded in scripture, however, turn out to be "interpretations of Hebrew (or Christian) faith: they did not really happen at all."

Soon others joined in. James Barr explicitly attacked Hoskyns' use of the *Wörterbuch* method in *Semantics of Biblical Language* in the same year as Gilkey's essay.[4] And later, in 1973, Barr wrote of the "modern revival of biblical theology" which characterized the forties and fifties as "a movement of the recent past":

> From the early sixties onward the climate of theology has drastically changed. The strongly authoritative type of theology, with its centre in the primacy of revelation, has lost its impetus and its leadership. Philosophical theology, as distinct from biblically based theology, has again increased in influence. Ideas which had been regarded as belonging to outmoded "liberalism" are being freely discussed again. It seems as if the great neo-orthodox revolution in theology had not taken place at all, so many of its favorite positions are denied or simply ignored.[5]

With Barr's assessment we may also compare Brevard Childs' contentions in his book *Biblical Theology in Crisis* (1970).[6] Childs has in view primarily the "American Biblical Theology Movement," an adjunct of the American neo-orthodoxy which arose in the 1940s, flourished in the 1950s, fell sick in the late 1950s, and died in the mid-1960s. But his judgments are equally applicable to the NT scholarship of Hoskyns in England.

Is Hoskyns' biblical theology justly described as a *détour?* In view of the 1981 publication of the doubly posthumous *Crucifixion-Resurrection*[7] and of the approaching centenary of Hoskyns' birth (1984), it would seem appropriate to ask whether this is an adequate assessment of his significance. I have two further reasons for wanting to do this. First, Hoskyns should be recognized as one of the progenitors of our society. Like Moses at Mount Pisgah, he did not live to see it, but his friendship with Gerhard Kittel was one of the factors that led to the planning of SNTS at the Oxford conference on Faith and Order. My second reason is one of personal *pietas.* Not only was I a pupil of Hoskyns in the last year of his life, but in 1938 I was the first (and only) exchange scholar to study at the Evangelisches Stift in Tübingen under a plan hatched by Hoskyns and Kittel. Then I spent a year at Queen's College Birmingham in 1939–40 where, as Lampe noted, Hoskyns' influence was also dominant.

Hoskyns' Life

The biographical details of Hoskyns' career are now readily accessible in Gordon Wakefield's excellent but all too brief memoir at the beginning of *Crucifixion-Resurrection,* and I need give only a brief summary of it here:

> Born 1884 at Notting Hill, London, the son of the Rev. Sir Edwyn Hoskyns, Bart., later Bishop of Southwell.
> Graduated from Cambridge with second class honors in the Historical Tripos in 1908.
> Studied in Berlin under Harnack 1908–1909.
> After a curacy, a wardenship of student hostel in Sheffield, and service as a chaplain in the British Army, he became Fellow and Dean of Corpus Christi College, Cambridge, in 1919. He served as Lecturer in the Divinity School of the university,

lecturing annually on the "Theology and Ethics of the New Testament."

Died 1937.

He published very little but enjoyed a wide influence through his writings and his teaching. The following works should be mentioned:

> "The Christ of the Synoptic Gospels" in *Essays Catholic and Critical* (1926).
>
> "Jesus the Messiah" in *Mysterium Christi* (1920). This is one of the papers read at the Eisenach-Canterbury series of Anglo-German conferences, which should be remembered as part of the *Vorgeschichte* of our society.
>
> *The Riddle of the New Testament,* in collaboration with his pupil F. N. Davey (1931). I saw this work translated into German, a rare event in those days, when I arrived in Tübingen in 1938. Its German title was *Das Rätsel des Neuen Testaments.* Hoskyns translated the revised edition of Karl Barth's *Römerbrief,* and it appeared in 1934. Apart from a few articles and reviews, especially in *JTS,* his other works were posthumous: *Cambridge Sermons* (ed. C. H. S. Smyth, 1938), *The Fourth Gospel* (ed. F. N. Davey, 1940), *We Are the Pharisees* (ed. F. N. Davey, 1960), *Crucifixion-Resurrection* (with F. N. Davey, 1981).

Hoskyns' academic qualifications were minimal, but his publications, though few, were very influential in their day, and perhaps still are. My purpose in the rest of this chapter will be to explore the question how far his work is dated and irrelevant today. This exploration will be based upon the works listed above.

What Is Biblical Theology?

As C. K. Barrett has recently recalled, when Hoskyns' pupils spoke of "theology" they meant "biblical theology."[8] But what did Hoskyns mean by the term? Barrett hoped we should know when *Crucifixion-Resurrection* appeared. But we look in vain for a systematic definition there. The nearest the authors come to discussing how it should be defined is in a chapter entitled "The Scope of Biblical Theology" (pp. 103–266). At least they make clear what it is not. They make no attempt to systematize the thought of the Bible under the traditional headings of dogmatic theology, nor do they try to systematize the thoughts of the individual writers of the New Testament. They refuse to do so because, so far as is known, they say, the first Christian believers themselves refused to do so. They did not "compress their insight into a system of theology or into a cosmic philosophy " (p. 209). "Paul did not, like some venerable scholastic, armed with a complete and mathematical system of reasoning, construct from the Scriptures an edifice of biblical theology" (p. 189). Rather, what we find in both Testaments is "a biblical pattern of insight that holds both Testaments together." It is the task of the biblical theologian to apprehend and to lay bare this pattern of insight. Davey, following Hoskyns' intention, proceeds to do this in Part II of *Crucifixion-Resurrection*. If they are prepared to talk of insights, they can also talk of themes: "The Poor—and the Poverty of Jesus"; "Father and Son—and the Dereliction of Jesus"; "Marriage—and the Isolation of Jesus"; "Government—and the Obedience of Jesus"; "Eating and Drinking—and the Self-Oblation of Jesus." It will be noted that each chapter involves a basic reality of human life: poverty and wealth, marriage and the family, eating and drinking, government and politics. And each finds in the Christ event the clue which makes sense of these activities and institutions. Doing biblical theology was thus for Hoskyns a matter of identifying the themes provided by these human realities and of relating them to the relevant facets of the Christ event or the gospel. For the Christ event and the gospel are God's answer which makes sense of it. During his lifetime people often discussed whether Hoskyns was a Barthian; he had translated Barth's *Römerbrief* from the sixth edition. In the context of the day, that usually meant, Did Hoskyns reject natural theology? I do not recollect ever discussing the subject, and I doubt whether he would have found it of interest. What he did maintain, however, is that the Bible contained important theological insights into the natural order. It is basically the

OT that points up the themes of human life, and it is the NT proclamation of the death and resurrection of Jesus which makes sense of them:

> This is the biblical setting in which the death and resurrection of Jesus is proclaimed, and in which Paul can speak of letter and spirit, of flesh and spirit, and of death and life (2 Cor. 5:15). If this setting be forgotten or misunderstood, the New Testament *does* degenerate into mythology, for it loses its basis in the Old Testament and has therefore lost its basis in the frank recognition of the actual poverty of human life when men "live unto themselves" (2 Cor. 5:15) or "of themselves" (2 Cor. 4:7), regarding life as a thing in itself expecting its own inherent perfectability, as the goal of their achievement or the source of their power (pp. 96–97).

The Bible thus pinpointed those universal aspects of the human condition which expose the finitude, weakness, and vulnerability of human being and then witnesses what God has done in the crucifixion and resurrection of Jesus to deal with that plight. Here human life is "finally affirmed and established and made good" (p. 206). We are not concerned with what Hoskyns frequently referred to as "propaganda imposed upon human life" but with the disclosure of a meaning embedded in the structure of life itself.

The Hermeneutical Gap

Since Hoskyns' time we have become much more concerned with the hermeneutical gap. Lampe is assuredly right that here we have taken up again a concern of which the older liberal Protestantism was aware but which was neglected during the biblical theology period. However, the problem presents itself differently today. The liberals thought there were certain outmoded concepts that could be jettisoned, such as the Virgin Birth, the miracles of Jesus, the empty tomb, and the literal ascension, leaving the rest intact. In Bultmann's demythologizing program, propounded after Hoskyns' death, the whole kerygma was seen to be couched in outmoded language and required translation. Hoskyns shows little awareness of this problem. Since Bultmann and since the new hermeneutic, a more radical view has been expressed by Dennis Nineham to the effect that the whole of the biblical material is so irretrievably conditioned by obsolete cultures that it is impossible to translate the biblical concepts intelligibly into contemporary conceptuality.[9] Hoskyns would have had a devastating critique of that position. The various cultural conditionings of the biblical material and present-day cultural conditioning he would have categorized as *sarx* (a favorite word, sometimes denoting human idolatry in fact of the truth of the living God), which has to be dethroned before it can be reestablished on a relative footing. However much modern life has changed, human beings are born, reared, fed, clothed, work; they succumb to sickness and death; and it is to these basic facts of human life, as real today as they were in NT times, that the gospel message was addressed.

Hoskyns was very much aware of a strangeness in the Bible, but its real strangeness arose not from its conditioning by cultures remote from our own, but from the message that was addressed to those cultures, and he believed, to ours as well. In an open letter to Karl Barth on the occasion of Barth's fiftieth birthday in 1936 Hoskyns wrote:

> For us, as for you in Central Europe, the subject matter of the Bible is difficult, strange and foreign. Yet in our aloofness we know that the relevance lies in its strangeness, and that we are involved in its definition of human life (*Cambridge Sermons*, p. 219).

I cannot help thinking that Hoskyns identified the strangeness of the Bible at a much deeper level than Nineham does. It lies not merely at the level of cultural differences. Hoskyns was of course aware of this level when he insisted on the importance of learning Greek to study the NT, but that was only relative and symbolic of the deeper difference between ourselves and the Bible. That deeper difference lay in the fact that the Bible delivered a message that was from outside all human culture. Nineham identifies only a superficial strangeness and therefore stigmatizes the biblical message as irrelevant; Hoskyns laid his finger on a deeper strangeness and found that precisely in that strangeness lay its relevance to all cultures.

Method in Biblical Theology

It is hard to say exactly what it was that died when people like Barr and Childs proclaim the death of "the biblical theology movement." As James Smart observed, there never was such a movement, and biblical theology is still being done today, even by Barr and Childs themselves. R. Hamerton-Kelly has distinguished between two basic methods by which biblical theology is currently being pursued.[10] There are those who take for its basic datum the testimony of the New Testament Christians and those who take for its base the events and persons to which the text testifies. In the first category belong R. Bultmann and his school, the American literary school (A. N. Wilder, and the SBL parable seminar), and although he is too complex to be ranged on one side, Paul Ricoeur. On the other side Hamerton-Kelly places W. Pannenberg as the most authoritative spokesman today. We might also include on this side E. Schillebeeckx, who in his two books *Jesus* and *Christ* clearly regards the historical Jesus as constitutive for NT Christology. Jesus' history for them is the norm and criterion of any interpretation of him. Hoskyns would have taken the side of Pannenberg and Schillebeeckx on this issue. In the introduction to *The Riddle of the New Testament,* Noel Davey, with Hoskyns' full approval (as throughout *The Riddle*), wrote:

> When the Catholic Christian kneels at the words *incarnatus est* or at the words *and was incarnate,* he marks with proper solemnity his recognition that the Christian Religion has its origin neither in general religious experience, nor in some peculiar esoteric mysticism, nor in a dogma, and he declares his faith to rest upon a particular event in history. Nor is the Catholic Christian peculiar in this concentration of faith. This is

Christian orthodoxy, both Catholic and Protestant. In consequence, the Christian religion is not merely open to historical investigation, but demands it, and its piety depends upon it. Inadequate or false reconstruction of the history of Jesus of Nazareth cuts at the heart of Christianity (p. 10).

To Hoskyns' pupils the "New Quest of the Historical Jesus" of the 1950s was not entirely new, though of course the critical tools employed by the New Quest were considerably sharper than those which were used in *The Riddle*. *The Riddle* is certainly aware of the distinction between the Jesus tradition and the redaction, as is shown in the chapters on the evangelists, on Matthew and Luke, and on Mark. But it assumes too readily that the Jesus behind the written gospel tradition is authentically historical, and does not employ explicit criteria to distinguish between the historical Jesus and the pre-gospel tradition. Instead, the method of *The Riddle* is to examine every unit of material of which the Gospels are composed (here Hoskyns was making limited use of the results of form criticism) such as miracles, parables, and aphorisms. *The Riddle* seeks to demonstrate that the very smallest units of which the gospel tradition is composed are "shot through with christological significance." Since the New Quest, many of us would want to say more cautiously that the material is shot through with *eschatological* significance and that it is only implicitly *christological*.

Yet it is interesting to find a recent book by a German author following very much along the lines of Hoskyns and Davey. W. Grimm, in his monograph, *Die Verkündigung Jesu und Deutero-Jesaja*,[11] seeks to show exactly as Hoskyns and Davey had done, though with much more technical equipment and with much greater thoroughness, that the sayings of Jesus are impregnated with OT material and especially with material from the later chapters of Isaiah. Independently of Hoskyns and Davey (whose work is not cited in the bibliography), Grimm finds for instance that the background of the Beelzebul sayings in Mark 3:27 is to be discovered in Isa. 49:24–25 (pp. 88–92); cf. *The Riddle of the New Testament*, p. 170). Moreover, *Crucifixion-Resurrection* has another striking parallel to Grimm, as the following passages will show.

The first is from *Crucifixion-Resurrection,* in the chapter entitled "The OT Setting of NT Theology." Having presented a number of Jesus logia, which are penetrated by the language of the OT,
Hoskyns and Davey conclude:

> Such passages represent far more than a mere citation of Old
> Testament texts, far more than an allusion to Old Testament
> language, far more than the application of Old Testament
> prophecy to substantiate the claims of Jesus. *This is a wholly
> creative handling that proceeds from a sure and certain understand-
> ing of it* [italics mine].

Hoskyns goes on to note how different is the evangelists' use of
the OT—a sort of application of the criterion of dissimilarity in
reverse:

> In narrating the life and death of Jesus, the synoptic evange-
> lists cast their narratives in words that recall Old Testament
> prophecy; they introduce citations to show explicit fulfil-
> ment; they were, no doubt, led to do so by a tradition origi-
> nating in the practice of Jesus himself. But there is a marked
> distinction between their pedestrian discovery of some de-
> gree of literal identity between the events they describe and
> Old Testament prophecy, and the confident assurance with
> which Jesus seizes upon a phrase of scripture, evokes its vast
> theological background. . . . They quote *because* he did,
> but not *as* he did.

We find a very similar conclusion drawn from Grimm's far more
extensive analysis of Jesus logia:

> Der atl. Hintergrund von Mark 3,27 bestätigt noch einmal,
> was schon die Darstellung der Evangelisten erkennen lässt:
> In den Dämonenaustreibungen geht es um das Heil des
> Menschen; sie sind nicht etwa ein Mirakel oder Demonstra-
> tion einer messianischen Macht, sondern eschatologische
> Rettungstat Gottes durch einen Gesandten, Antwort auf die
> Not des Menschen, nicht Befriedigung seiner Wundersucht
> (p. 22).

Grimm also notes the failure of the evangelists to measure up to the insight of Jesus into the OT material. On the closely related Q-logion Matt. 11:12/Luke 16:16 he observes:

> Lk hat das Q-logion nicht mehr verstanden und seinen atl. Hintergrund nicht mehr erkannt (p. 96).

In discussing the Beatitudes, Grimm similarly notes how the evangelists progressively lost sight of the Deutero-Isaianic background of Jesus' logia:

> Jesu Botschaft war doch offenbar stärker noch von Dtjes bestimmt, als es den Evangelisten bewusst war.

Both Hoskyns and Grimm find a background for the seed parables of Mark 4 in Isa. 55:10f. Hoskyns (*Riddle,* p. 185) quotes Isa. 55:10f. to show that the metaphor of sowing in the OT "almost demanded a Messianic application" (ibid.).

Similarly Grimm writes:

> Die Gleichnisse vom Säemann (Mk. 4.3–8), von der selbstwachsenden Saat (V. 26–29) und vom Senfkorn (V. 30–32) haben mit Jes. 55. 10 f.; 61.11 neben sprachlichen Berührungen eine auffallende Ähnlichkeit im Bildmaterial, in formaler Hinsicht, ja sogar in der durch den Zusammenhang betimmten Aussage (p. 133).

In evaluating the significance of Jesus' use of Deutero-Isaianic material, Hoskyns and Davey come to the conclusion that this warrants the assumption that Jesus' ministry was "messianic" or christological in its significance:

> The aphorisms of Jesus, then, cannot be detached from this Messianic background, and they cannot be detached from the particular happening in Palestine. They . . . are rooted in a peculiar Messianic history. The peculiar Christology penetrates the aphoristic teaching of Jesus as it penetrates the record of His miracles and of His parables. The Christology

lies behind the aphorisms, not ahead of them; this means
that at no point is the literal or historical critic able to detect
in any stratum of the Synoptic material evidence that a
Christological interpretation has been imposed upon an un-
Christological history (*Riddle*, p. 207).

Before we too hastily dismiss this conclusion as pre–form critical,
we should note that W. Grimm in the post–form critical era has
drawn precisely the same conclusion from an examination of the
same stock of Jesus tradition:

> Jesus hat verschiedenen Ebed-Stellen auf den Inhalt seiner
> Sendung bezogen. Die Ebed-Bezeichnung war als solche
> ganz gewiss nicht entscheidend für Jesu Selbstverständ-
> nis . . . ; nicht von ungefähr fehlt sie in Jesusworten ganz.
> Doch war die dtjes. Botschaft insgesamt allerdings grundle-
> gen für die endzeitliche Aufgabe Jesu und—wenn man
> will—für seine Messianität (p. 311).

"Wenn man will"—that is the problem raised by the conclusion
both of Hoskyns-Davey and of Grimm. Can we subscribe to that
unqualified application of "messianic" or "christological" to the
historical Jesus? Most of us would find it more fitting to speak of
an "implicit" or "indirect" Christology in the historical Jesus material (Conzelmann, Bornkamm). What *is* explicit in the pre-
Easter Jesus is a "theology of Jesus" (Schillebeeckx), that is, the
conviction that God is speaking and acting through him; and insofar as there is any self-reflection in Jesus, it is in terms of eschatological prophecy. In referring to Jesus' prophetic consciousness as
an example of a "theology of Jesus," A. E. Harvey,[12] writing in
1982, speaks of the earthly Jesus as the one who appeared as
"God's agent." That would seem to be a much safer judgment than
that rather loose and undefined talk about "messianic" and
"christological" that we find in Hoskyns and Davey and about
Messianität in Grimm. Yet I am not sure that Hoskyns would not
in the last analysis have agreed. He does not base his attribution of
messiahship to Jesus so much upon the overt use of the messianic
titles as upon the inner substance of his sayings and deeds. In this

sense Hoskyns regarded the messianic secret as something embedded in the actual history of Jesus, not, as the form and redaction critics repeatedly insist, to be found exclusively in the Marcan redaction: "Das Messiasgeheimnis gehört nicht zur Tradition, sondern zur redaktionellen Arbeit des Mk."[13] As Hoskyns-Davey saw it, there was a profound reason in Jesus' history for Mark's redactional presentation of the messianic secret:

> It is no doubt attractive to suppose that the contradictions in the Gospels constitute but another illustration of the intrusion of the later faith of the Church into the historical tradition; or in this case, of the later doctrine of the secret Messiahship of Jesus (*Crucifixion-Resurrection,* p. 221).

From this the two authors go on to find the roots of that later doctrine in the historical "poverty" of Jesus. In *The Riddle* they had spoken similarly of the "humiliation" of Jesus as the historical root of the later doctrine of the messianic secret:

> Although Mark presumes and indeed insists that Jesus is in fact the Son of God, and arranges his material to lead men to the conception of Jesus which the title expresses, he deliberately tries to show that a true understanding of His Sonship can be reached only through the recognition of His humiliation, completed in the Crucifixion, and vindicated by His Raising from the dead.

From Mark, Hoskyns and Davey press back to the pre-gospel tradition and thence to the logia and acts of Jesus himself to show that this hidden messiahship was present in the actual history. And they conclude, "At no point is the literary or historical critic able to detect in any stratum of the Synoptic material evidence that a Christological interpretation has been imposed upon an un-Christological history" (*Riddle,* p. 207). Yet this Christology is to be found, not in the outward use of christological titles by Jesus himself, but in the impregnation of his logia by OT language and imagery and in the poverty and humiliation of his life. The Hoskyns-Davey position on the messianic secret is remarkably close to, though quite independent of, that of Julius Schniewind (Dr. H. W. Bartsch first suggested to me in conversation the similarities between Hoskyns and Schniewind). Schniewind wrote in his commentary on Mark:

> Jesus ist schon auf Erden der Messias, der Gotteskönig, aber im Geheimen, Verborgenen.—W. Wrede, der als Erster das Messias-Geheimnis, beobachtete, hielt all diese Züge für Übermalung des ursprünglichen Jesus-Bildes. Aber es wird sich zeigen, dass hinter jeder Erzählung und jedem Jesus-Wort unserer Evangelien dies Geheimnis steht.[14]

This understanding of the christological nature of the original Jesus history provides a response to Langdon Gilkey's gravamen against the biblical theology of the second decade of this century, namely, its talk about the "mighty acts" of God. The mighty acts of God for biblical theologians like Hoskyns or Schniewind are to be found precisely, and paradoxically, in the obscurity of the original history. The mighty acts of God are discernible in the history only to the eyes of faith. The miraculous "Übermalung" of the original exodus history in the light of Israel's covenant faith and of the pre-Easter Jesus in the light of the Easter faith are attempts to lay bare the inner meaning of the original history:

> It was the circumstances of his death—the behaviour of the crowds, of the authorities, Jewish and imperial, above all of Jesus himself—and those things that took place immediately afterwards, that enabled the apostles to understand what Jesus had previously said and done (*Crucifixion-Resurrection*, p. 223).

The "mighty acts" of God were not immediately apprehensible as such while they were occurring but only in the light of their completion as perceived in faith. This is not an uneasy combination of liberalism and orthodoxy, as Langdon Gilkey thought, but an attempt to do justice to the double aspect of the Gospels, which on the one hand portray Jesus in his hiddenness and humiliation and on the other hand bring out the epiphanic character of the history. A French Canadian scholar has recently made a similar point:

> Jésus passa parmi les siens presque incognito. Il se révéla sans ostentation ni grandeur mondaines. . . . Ses disciples, durant sa vie terrestre, perçurent à l'occasion, comme en un éclair, son mystère. Mais ce fût sa resurrection d'entre les morts qui l'authentifia vraiment à leurs yeux comme le Messie de Dieu et le fils d l'homme.[15]

Here we may recall the difference between Bultmann and Käse-mann over the Christology of John. Bultmann stressed that the Word became *flesh* as an act of humiliation and condescension. Käsemann in the *Testament of Jesus* (1968, esp. pp. 8–9) rejected this Christology of humiliation as an imposition of Pauline Christology upon the Fourth Gospel and insisted that the Johannine Christ is portrayed as a God striding upon the earth: the stress was to be laid on "we behold his glory." I think Hoskyns would have held both views in tension. On the one hand, the humiliation of the Christos is not merely given a nodding assent in John 1:14 or in the appendix to the eucharistic discourse in John 6:51–58, but is found at the very heart of the discourse material in the Father/Son Christology, as Hoskyns and Davey have brought out clearly in the best chapter of *Crucifixion-Resurrection,* the one entitled "Father and Son—and the Dereliction of Jesus" (pp. 227–39). Here the two authors find the core of Johannine Christology in the Father's sending of the Son and the Son's obedience to the Father:

> The relation between father and son is not described as a dumb transmission of life and behaviour. It is a tradition or handing over of teaching and commandment. The father commands, the son obeys. Obedience is therefore the characteristic note of sonship. A son reproduces that behaviour of his father because he hears and obeys. . . . Here again, it is in the fourth Gospel that this rhythm of obedience is most precisely formulated:

> The Son can do nothing of himself, but what he seeth the
> Father doing. (John 5:19)
>
> I can of myself do nothing; as I hear I judge. I seek not
> my own will, but the will of him that sent me. (John
> 5:30)
>
> As I have kept my Father's commandment and abide in
> his love. (John 15:15)
> (*Crucifixion-Resurrection*, p. 232).

And what of the cross in the Fourth Gospel? Is it, as Käsemann
argued, retained simply as a concession to tradition, without any
integral place in the Johannine view of revelation? Hoskyns and
Davey, in their chapter in *Crucifixion-Resurrection* entitled "The
Death of Jesus in the Fourth Gospel" (pp. 133–54), set out to
demonstrate that for the Fourth Evangelist the death of Jesus was
indeed the clue to every revelatory word and deed in the earlier
part of the Gospel. And so "the death of Jesus is the 'place,' the sole
place of understanding" (p. 152). The Johannine emphasis on the
glory of the *Christos* is not, as Käsmann thought, the product of a
"naive docetism," but a paradoxical reality revealed in the cross.

Lower and Higher Christology

Since Hoskyns' time we have learned to draw a sharper distinction
not only between the implicit Christology of the historical Jesus
and the explicit Christology of the post-Easter community, but also
between the lower Christology of the earliest community and the
higher Christology of the later NT writers. In the lower Christology, Jesus was the human agent of God's salvific activity (A. E.
Harvey). Jesus had a "theology of Jesus" (Schillebeeckx) rather than
a christological self-understanding. In the later Christology, the
ego of Jesus becomes ontologically continuous with the preexistent
wisdom, or logos, of God conceived as sharing the very being of
God himself. Hoskyns and Davey were not unaware of the difference between the lower and higher Christologies. They can antici-
pate Harvey in speaking of Jesus as the Agent of God (*Riddle,*

p. 42). They are also aware that Paul, the Johannine writings, and Hebrews place an "emphasis" on the preexistence of Jesus which is not found in the earlier writings. But they do not see any real contradiction here. In his commentary on the Fourth Gospel, when he deals with the prologue, Hoskyns refuses to attribute this shift of emphasis to extraneous influences: "The workshop in which the Word of God was forged to take its natural place among the great theological descriptions of Jesus and His work is a Christian workshop: the tools are Christian tools."[16] Before the history of religions scholars reject this view as inconsistent with the state of the evidence, let them reflect on what exactly Hoskyns is claiming. From the very first in his sayings and deeds Jesus uttered God's eschatological words to Israel. To those who accepted his message, Jesus was from the first regarded as the eschatological embodiment of the Word of God. "The figure of Jesus as the embodiment of the Word of God controls the whole matter of the Christian religion" (*The Fourth Gospel,* p. 163). Here is a salutary warning, as relevant today as when it was first put forward. When we have demonstrated the sources of NT images and concepts in extraneous religions and philosophies, we have not yet reached a theological understanding of their Christian use. This can be achieved only from their referent, the Jesus event itself. Hoskyns would therefore have argued that the "higher Christology" of the later NT strata, far from being a dubious and dispensable development, is in fact a necessary clarification of the earlier tradition, with no essential difference of meaning. Incarnational Christology is thus in legitimate continuity with the earlier divine agent Christology.

Eschatology and Apocalyptic

Johann Christiaan Beker, in his work *Paul the Apostle,* has recently argued that the basic emphasis in biblical theology should be placed not upon the past event of Jesus but on the future triumph of God in the *parousia.*[17] Hoskyns on the contrary laid almost exclusive emphasis on the past, on what had already been achieved in the Christ event. He dealt with this question at some length in one of

his Cambridge sermons during a course entitled "Eschatology." He
began that course with a description of the excitement occasioned
by an incident one Sunday morning at a service in the fell country
of Westmoreland. Crowds were flocking to the church—not a
usual sight in modern England, as Hoskyns wryly observed. The
excitement was caused by the preacher's message. The world was
coming to an end and Christ would return at any moment. In his
sermon Hoskyns set out to counter future apocalyptic (he had Albert Schweitzer in mind) by offering an interpretation in terms of
its realization in the life of the Christian ecclesia:

> Paul is using eschatological language to describe a present and
> concrete experience. The stars do not fall, nor do the moun-
> tains crumble away, the sun still shines and the stars continue
> to twinkle. The physical structure of the universe remains,
> but the dream of righteousness and peace and holiness and
> knowledge which hitherto belonged to the eschatological
> hope, has become a concrete reality, and the Christians stand
> within this New Order of the Spirit, and the two worlds of
> the flesh and of the Spirit, of this world and of the world be-
> yond, become not two periods of human history but one
> sacramental living whole.[18]

This is pretty close to what Beker calls the "divine common-
wealth" realized eschatology of Ephesians, whose dominance in
neo-orthodoxy he so roundly condemns (Beker, p. 142). Elsewhere, however, Hoskyns does show himself more open to the
"noch nicht." He can, for instance, interpret the first beatitude in
futuristic terms: "'Blessed are the poor, for theirs is the kingdom
of God' cannot mean in its context that the oppressed possess the
Kingdom now because they are poor. It must mean that those who
are conscious of oppression need not despair, since the future belongs to them and not to their oppressors" (Cambridge Sermons,
p. 17). But this "noch nicht" is undeveloped. Hoskyns was very
much a figure of his age, the age of Barth, Bultmann, and C. H.
Dodd, all of whom in various ways tended to allow the future aspect
of eschatology to be swallowed up in present realization, whether
pietistically, ecclesially, or existentially interpreted. Clearly, the

"noch nicht" has to be taken much more seriously than any of these writers allow. But this does not mean that with Beker the major emphasis should be shifted to the future consummation. This seems to result in a re-Judaizing of the gospel, the distinctiveness of which must assuredly lie in the Jesus event, the *geschehenes Geschehen,* however much it still cries out for future consummation. Hoskyns was basically right in placing primary emphasis on the Jesus event though inadequate in his recognition of the necessity of the "noch nicht." In any case, he was dealing with an issue which is still very much alive today.

Conclusion

Hoskyns' biblical theology was fragmentary, largely intuitive, and in many ways dated. Since his time new methods (e.g., redaction criticism, structuralism, etc.) have emerged, and new issues have arisen. One need only mention demythologizing and existential interpretation, the new quest of the historical Jesus, and the new hermeneutic.

Hoskyns would not have expected his theology to last forever. He had to establish his own position over against the liberal Protestantism and Anglican Catholic modernism of his day. In doing so, he recognized that each generation has to work out its own theology for itself: "The assured results of the previous generation require constant reconsideration when seen in a new perspective" (*Riddle,* p. 13). But as Gordon Wakefield, the editor of *Crucifixion-Resurrection,* observed, "Because Hoskyns was wrestling with the same biblical texts as we are, and immersed in the problems of the same humanity, it is more than probable that something of what he wrote will speak to our world." At the same time, Wakefield himself deliberately eschewed any attempt to bring Hoskyns into dialogue with more recent scholarship. That task I have attempted to undertake here. The unfinished agenda of the older liberal theology has certainly acquired fresh urgency since the 1960s, but it would hardly be wise to approach that agenda as though Hoskyns and his biblical theology were merely a *détour.*

Notes

1. For a critique of the term "biblical theology movement," see James D. Smart, *The Past, Present and Future of Biblical Theology* (Philadelphia: Westminster Press, 1979), esp. chap. 1, "The 'Movement' That Was Not a Movement," pp. 9–17.

2. Geoffrey W. H. Lampe, "Salvation: Traditions and Reappraisals," *Queen's Essays* (Birmingham: Queen's College, 1980), 63–80. Cf. Alan Wilkinson in *Theology* 6 (1983): 114: "I have since realized that the radicals of the 60s were in effect tackling the unfinished theological business and ethical agenda created by the First World War, but evaded by neo-orthodoxy."

3. J. Langdon Gilkey, "Cosmology, Ontology, and the Travail of Biblical Language," *JR* (1961): 194–205.

4. James Barr, *Semantics of Biblical Language* (Oxford: Oxford University Press, 1961), 195–97.

5. James Barr, *The Bible in the Modern World* (New York: Harper & Row, 1973), 5.

6. Brevard Childs, *Biblical Theology in Crisis* (Philadelphia: Westminster Press, 1970), esp. 61–87.

7. Edwyn Clement Hoskyns and Francis Noel Davey, *Crucifixion-Resurrection* (London: SPCK, 1981). This doubly posthumous work is scrappy, ill-organized, and incomplete, but, as we hope to show, contains brilliant flashes of insight.

8. C. K. Barrett, "What Is New Testament Theology? Some Reflections," *Horizons in Biblical Theology* 3 (1981): 1–22.

9. Dennis Nineham, *The Use and Abuse of the Bible: A Study of the Bible in an Age of Rapid Cultural Change,* Library of Philosophy and Religion (London: Macmillan & Co., 1976), 1–39.

10. R. Hamerton-Kelly, *God the Father: Theology and Patriarchy in the Teaching of Jesus,* Overtures to Biblical Theology (Philadelphia: Fortress Press, 1979), esp. "An Excursus on Method: Symbol and History in Modern Hermeneutics," pp. 105–22.

11. W. Grimm, *Die Verkündigung Jesu und Deutero-Jesaja,* ANTJ 1 (Frankfurt am Main/Bern: Lang, ²1981).

12. A. E. Harvey, *Jesus and the Constraints of History* (Philadelphia: Westminster Press, 1982), 258.

13. H. Conzelmann–A. Lindemann, *Arbeitsbuch des Neuen Testaments* (Tübingen: J. C. B. Mohr, ⁶1982), 258.

14. Julius Schniewind, *Das Evangelium nach Markus,* NTD 1 (Göttingen: Vandenhoeck & Ruprecht, ⁵1949), 55.

15. G. Rochais, *Les récits de résurrection des morts dans le Nouveau Testament,* SNTSMS 40 (Cambridge: Cambridge University Press, 1981), 166.

16. Edwyn Clement Hoskyns, *The Fourth Gospel,* vol. 1, ed. F. N. Davey (London: Faber & Faber, ¹1940), 162–63.

17. Johann Christiaan Beker, *Paul the Apostle: The Triumph of God in Life and Thought* (Philadelphia: Fortress Press, 1980).

18. Edwyn Clement Hoskyns, *Cambridge Sermons* (London: SPCK, 1938), 26–27.

PART TWO

The Historical Jesus

2

THE CLUE TO JESUS'
SELF-UNDERSTANDING

Any attempt to discover how Jesus understood his mission, and therefore his own person, is bound to come to grips with the messianic and other titles attributed to him in the Gospels. We will restrict ourselves here to some of the sayings of Jesus in which he himself predicates of himself such titles. We will not concern ourselves with the use of these titles on the lips of others, whether in confession of faith (as at Caesarea Philippi) or in hostile examination (as in the high priest's question at the trial). Nor will we concern ourselves with the indirect disclosure of Jesus' self-understanding to be found in his proclamation of the reign of God, in his enunciation of the radical demand of obedience, in his teaching on the immediacy of God's fatherly care, and his actions in calling disciples to follow him, in eating with publicans and sinners, in healing the sick and casting out demons, or in exposing himself to death through his final journey to Jerusalem, though all these words and works are of fruitful consequence in the attempt to establish Jesus' self-understanding, and actually of more conclusive nature than the discussion of the messianic titles. We restrict ourselves to these because here, if anywhere, Jesus' self-understanding would become explicit.

In the study of the synoptists, six messianic titles come into question: Christ, Lord, Son of David, Son or Son of God, Servant of the Lord, and Son of man. Of these we can at once eliminate Christ, Lord, and Son of David on either source-critical or form-critical grounds or both. Even if it be argued, as it can be, that Jesus echoes servant language, there is, as is well known,[1] no explicit self-identification with the servant. Self-identification with the Son or Son of God is surprisingly rare. It has indeed the merit of occurring in both primary sources Mark and Q, but it occurs in both only once, Matt. 11:27 para. (the cry of jubilation) and in the Markan apocalypse (Mark 13:32). The first passage has long been under fire as a Hellenistic product, and even if we do not agree with this estimate, its postresurrection liturgical character seems beyond doubt. The apocalyptic passage is probably, as I have argued elsewhere,[2] indicative of an original Son of man. This is not really a case of agreement between Mark and Q.

When we come to the term *Son of man* we are on much firmer ground. Its use is firmly embedded in the logia of Jesus and is found in both primary strata of the Gospels, Mark and Q. There is, however, one qualification to be made: the sayings which speak of the suffering Son of man are found only in the Markan material and are therefore not so well attested as the other two groups, those which identify Jesus in his present activity with the Son of man and those which speak of the future coming of the transcendental Son of man. These types of Son of man sayings are found in both primary strata and to this extent are assured. Turning from the test of source criticism to that of form criticism, we are left with an uncertain answer. Here the criterion of authenticity is whether or not a saying reflects the theology of the postresurrection church. If it does, then the saying in question should, provisionally at least, be put to the credit of the postresurrection church, rather than to the earthly Jesus. This is of course not an absolute criterion, for it is conceivable that Jesus and the early postresurrection church were in agreement. But it is better to err on the side of caution. The question is, Did the postresurrection church confess Jesus as Son of man? The answer is not quite as conclusive as is sometimes supposed, at least in Britain. It is true that in the Gospels the title is reserved exclusively to the logia of Jesus, a fact which weighs strongly with British scholars. On the other hand it is found in Acts 7:56, a circumstance which led Cullmann into a curious inconsistency in his *Christology of the New Testament.* He professes to accept the form-critical method. On the one hand he attributes the Son of man Christology specifically to the Stephanic circle,[3] and yet on the other hand he accepts without question the authenticity of the Son of man logia. In addition, there is the Pauline use of *anthropos* and Adam of Jesus in Rom. 5, 1 Cor. 15 (cf. 1 Tim. 2:5) which is widely thought to be an idiomatic rendering of the semitic *bar nasha.* Next, there is the application of Ps. 8:5 to Jesus in Heb. 2:6 and finally the application of Dan. 7:13 in Rev. 1:13. If this is thought to be strong enough evidence that the early church did confess or proclaim Jesus as Son of man after the resurrection, then form-critical method would bid us lay aside all the Son of man sayings. But the problem is not so simply disposed of as that.

It was rather a shock when Bultmann[4] pointed out that within the sayings which speak of the future coming of the transcendental Son of man there are one or two which quite palpably distinguish between the earthly Jesus and the future, transcendent Son of man. This led Bultmann of course to conclude that Jesus did speak of the Son of man, and as of one different from himself; to interpret all the other future Son of man sayings in this sense, and to regard these alone as authentic. It led him to the notorious statement "the life of Jesus was unmessianic." The conclusion so shocked British scholars that they have on the whole rejected even Bultmann's interpretation of Mark 8:38, Luke 12:8f. In my book, *The Mission and Achievement of Jesus,*[5] I argued that this distinction provided an important clue for Jesus' use of the Son of man. Professor Richardson, in his *Introduction to the Theology of the New Testament,* castigated me for following Bultmann at this point ("Even the sure-footed Fuller stumbled here," he wrote)[6] and rejected Bultmann's interpretation out of hand, though without really refuting it.

I think Bultmann is undoubtedly right in this interpretation, though, as I will show, there is no need to follow him in the skeptical conclusions that he draws from it. The distinction between

Jesus and the Son of man has highly positive implications for Jesus' self-understanding.

Before embarking upon the major thesis of this chapter, I must however briefly trace the course of discussion since Bultmann (N. B.: Dr. A. J. B. Higgins, in his *Forschungsbericht*[7] on the study of the Son of man since 1931, published in the memorial volume to T. W. Manson edited by him, has said next to nothing of this most significant discussion within the Bultmann school). There is continued agreement with the master in the rejection of the present and suffering sayings as authentic logia of the earthly Jesus, though there is a trend to seek a different creative milieu for them. Bornkamm[8] thinks that the present sayings are purely postresurrection creations of the church—Bultmann it will be remembered denied they were messianic and held that originally they meant "child of man," that is, man in general. Bornkamm's acceptance of their messianic character involves the rejection of their authenticity. Tödt[9] in his painstaking analysis of all the Son of man logia in the synoptic tradition agrees that the suffering Son of man sayings are nonauthentic; but whereas Bultmann ascribes them to the Hellenistic church and probably to the evangelist Mark, Tödt attributes them to the Palestinian church. With regard to the future Son of man sayings, there is a division of opinion in the Bultmann school. There are some (Bornkamm,[10] Fuchs,[11] and Tödt[12]) who agree with Bultmann and accept the authenticity at least of some of those which explicitly distinguish between Jesus and the Son of man. We might call these the right-wing post-Bultmannians. And there are others (Käsemann,[13] Conzelmann,[14] and particularly Vielhauer[15]) who regard *all* the future sayings as creations of the postresurrection church, so that Jesus never used the term Son of man, not even of another. This apparent out-Bultmanning Bultmann is not, however, due to excessive skepticism. On the contrary it is the result of a reluctance to admit that Jesus could have envisaged any other figure coming after himself, so impressed are these post-Bultmannians by the immediate presence of God's eschatological word in Jesus and by what they call his "implicit" or "indirect" Christology. The evidence for this they find not in the use of titles (which would be direct Christology) but variously in his eschatological message and call to decision, in his conduct in eating with publicans and sinners, and so forth.

Now it must be admitted that even if we followed the left-wing post-Bultmannians, we should have sufficient evidence to establish a real continuity between the self-understanding of Jesus and his interpretation in messianic categories in the church's kerygma. The resurrection encounters vindicated Jesus' eschatological message and made his implicit self-understanding explicit.

At the same time, however, there are grounds for refusing to follow the left-wing post-Bultmannians in their denial to Jesus of such passages as Mark 8:38, Luke 12, 8 para. First, that denial overlooks the unique character of these sayings, namely, the palpable distinction between Jesus and the Son of man. If, as the post-Bultmannians, both right and left wing, are entirely agreed, the postresurrection church identified Jesus with the Son of man, we have here a clear instance of sayings which differ from the kerygma of the post–Easter church, and there is therefore no reason, on grounds of form criticism, for denying their authenticity.

Second, Vielhauer, repeating (though independently) an argument already used by the American scholar H. B. Sharman[16] in his book *The Son of Man and the Kingdom of God,* points out that Jesus' logia of the kingdom of God never introduce the concept of the Son of man, and the Son of man logia never introduce the concept of the kingdom of God. From this, Vielhauer deduces that the Son of man and the kingdom of God logia derive from different strata in the tradition. Since it is universally agreed that Jesus did use the concept of the kingdom of God, it follows that the concept of the Son of man must be denied to him and ascribed rather to the church.

Against this it may be argued that it is most unlikely that the early church should have introduced on such a large scale and in such very different usages the concept of the Son of man into the logia of Jesus unless there was some starting point within the genuine logia for the growth of such a tradition at such an early date (the overlapping of Mark and Q!). Moreover, the dissociation of the two concepts is perhaps to be explained from the circumstance that the kingdom of God formed the subject of Jesus' *public* proclamation, whereas the Son of man logia were addressed precisely to these who had already obeyed his call "follow me" and thus had adhered not only to his message, but also to his person as the embodiment of his message. The terms of Mark 8:38, Luke 12:8f. presuppose such an adherence to Jesus' person and must therefore have been addressed to the inner circle of his disciples. This is, I know, an argument employed for related though different purposes by the late T. W. Manson,[17] and as used by him it was vulnerable in that it depended on the present contexts. These contexts, however, are the creation of the evangelists themselves or of the oral tradition before them. They have no historical trustworthiness. As used here, the argument depends on the intrinsic *content* of the logia in question, *not on their context.*

We may therefore safely assume the authenticity of Mark 8:38, Luke 12:8f. They are doubly attested (Mark and Q), and they pass the test of form criticism. Now let us take a closer look at these sayings.

> Mark 8:38 reads:
>> If anyone is ashamed of me and my (words)
>>> in this wicked and godless age,
>> The Son of man will be ashamed of him
>>> when he comes in the glory of his Father and of the
>>> holy angels.
>
> Luke 12:8f.:
>> Everyone who acknowledges me before men
>>> the Son of man will acknowledge before the angels
>>> of God,
>> But he who disowns me before men
>>> will be disowned before the angels of God.
>
> cf. Matt. 10:32f.
>> Whoever then will acknowledge me before men
>>> I will acknowledge before my Father in heaven;
>> And whoever disowns me before men,
>>> I will disown before my Father in heaven.

It is clear that we have here one single logion which has undergone various changes in the tradition. In the Q version it is a double logion of clear poetic structure: A–B; A–B. The first part is positive, "acknowledge-acknowledge," and the second part negative, "disown-disown." The antithetic parallelism here suggests that the longer Q form of the saying is original, and that the Markan form has been shorn of the preceding positive part, perhaps because of its context—Mark 8:37.

There is a striking difference between the Lukan and the Matthean form of the Q saying. The Lukan form preserves clearly in the first part the distinction between Jesus and the Son of man. The Matthean has obliterated it by substituting the first person singular for the Son of man in each of the second quarters (the transcendental parts) of the saying. Clearly, Matthew is a secondary modification, adopted to bring the saying in line with the church's identification of Jesus with the Son of man. That it was felt necessary to make this change would seem to be a further indication of the pre-Easter origin of the logion in its original form.

The third point to be noted is that in the second negative part of the Lukan version of the Q saying the term *Son of man* has been removed and a reverential periphrasis substituted: "will be disowned before the angels of God." Perhaps this is Vielhauer's[18] strongest argument: that the saying, while authentic, did not contain the term *Son of man* but only a reverential periphrasis, reminiscent of the close of the parables of the lost sheep and lost coin: "there is joy in the presence of the angels of God over one sinner who repents" (Luke 15:10, cf. 15:7). On the other hand, it is to be noted that the decapitated Markan form, which preserves only the negative part, contains "Son of man," and therefore its presence in the negative part of the saying before Mark and Q traditions began to diverge seems assured.

The fourth point to be noticed is that the Markan tradition has begun the process of apocalyptic embroidery when it speaks of the "glory" of the Son of man. Further secondary traits are the use of the term *Father* for God (not that we would deny that Jesus spoke of God as Father, but this, once established, is more likely to have been introduced at other places). Third, the apocalyptic trinity "Father, Son of man, angels" is a further apocalyptic elaboration. One final point: Mark has "ashamed," whereas the Q tradition has "disown."

Tödt[19] is probably right in regarding "ashamed" as a Paulinism, or at least a characteristic word of the Hellenistic church.

We conclude therefore that the original form of the saying was as follows:

> Everyone who acknowledges me before men
>> The Son of man will acknowledge before the angels of God;
> But he who disowns me before men
>> The Son of man will him disown before the angels of God.

The first thing to notice in this logion is the reduction of the apocalyptic element to the absolute minimum. Here is no *parousia* on the clouds of heaven, no elaborate judgment scene, but only the appearance of the Son of man as advocate before the heavenly court. Clearly, Jesus is completely uninterested in the Son of man for his own sake. He is not giving apocalyptic prophecy about the coming Son of man, however reduced, as even Bultmann seems to imagine. The weight of emphasis rests rather on the first part of the logion, on the present, rather than on the future, on the infinite significance of acknowledging or disowning Jesus in this present. Adherence to Jesus in this present age is decisive for one's participation in the future eschatological salvation. Rejection of Jesus in this present age is deprivation of eschatological salvation in the future. Jesus introduces the Son of man merely as a rubber stamp to confirm the salvation which he already in the present mediates. Jesus does not identify himself with the rubber stamp, but the rubber stamp is brought in solely for his sake. Recognition of the distinction between Jesus and the Son of man does not necessarily result in a negative, skeptical conclusion with regard to Jesus' self-understanding. It does not mean that Jesus' self-understanding was ultimately nonmessianic. For if it was nonmessianic in expression (and with this we are prepared to agree), it was not nonmessianic in substance, if we are using *messianic* as a broad term for the bringer of eschatological salvation.

We might put it like this: While Jesus does not express a messianic self-consciousness in any of the accepted messianic categories, he does have something which comes pretty close to an incarnation consciousness. Here in him is: "God's presence and his very self," not substantially but actively. Of course, the term *incarnation* and the framework of thought which it implies was alien to Jesus as it was to post-Easter Palestinian Judaism. It became possible only in Hellenistic Christianity, and its source is another problem. There were no categories which spoke of preexistence and katabasis, nor was there any need for them. But what that mythology expresses is expressed by Jesus in a different way when he asserts the decisive significance of his person and of adherence to his person for a man's future eschatological salvation. For all its mythological overtones, the Johannine prologue is as close as it could be to the historical Jesus when it says: "The Word was made flesh and dwelt among us." For Jesus understood himself as the one through whom God was uttering his last eschatological word to Israel, by which men's salvation or damnation would be decided. He understood himself as the one in whom God was decisively and eschatologically at work. The resurrection does not create this assessment of Jesus. It restores it after it had been radically called in question by the cross. Once restored, it is, however, restated in terms of an explicit Christology. Jesus is identified with the coming Son of man. Because he is risen he has now vindicated himself. He is his own rubber stamp. Only to this extent may we speak of discontinuity between the self-understanding of Jesus and the messianic assessment of his person in the kerygma.

Notes

1. W. Manson, *Jesus the Messiah* (London: Hodder & Stoughton, 1943), 111.

2. R. H. Fuller, *The Mission and Achievement of Jesus* (London: SCM Press, 1954), 83.

3. O. Cullmann, *The Christology of the New Testament* (Philadelphia: Westminster Press, 1959), 165.

4. R. Bultmann, *Theology of the New Testament,* vol. 1 (London: SCM Press, 1952), 29.

5. Fuller, *Mission and Achievement,* 101f.

6. Alan Richardson, *Introduction to the Theology of the New Testament* (London: SCM Press, 1958), 134.

7. A. J. B. Higgins, "Son of Man-Forschung Since 'The Teaching of Jesus,'" in *New Testament Essays,* ed. A. J. B. Higgins (Manchester: University of Manchester Press, 1959), 119–35; see esp. n. 24, p. 133, for a slight reference to Bornkamm.

8. G. Bornkamm, *Jesus of Nazareth* (London/New York: Harper & Brothers, 1960), esp. 229.

9. H. E. Tödt, *Der Menschensohn in der synoptischen Überlieferung* (Gütersloh: Mohn, 1959), 131ff. and 250ff.

10. Bornkamm, *Jesus,* 228.

11. E. Fuchs, *ZTK* 55 (1958): 181.

12. Tödt, *Menschensohn,* 37ff., 50f.

13. E. Käsemann, *ZTK* 51 (1954): 149f.

14. H. Conzelmann, "Jesus Christus," *RGG*[3] 3 (1958): 630f.

15. P. Vielhauer, "Gottesreich und Menschensohn in der Verkündigung Jesu," in Festschrift für G. Dehn (Neukirchen: Erziehungsverlag, 1957), 51–79.

16. H. B. Sharman, *The Son of Man and the Kingdom of God* (Chicago: University of Chicago Press, 1944).

17. T. W. Manson, *The Teaching of Jesus,* 2d ed. (Cambridge: Cambridge University Press, 1935), 213f.

18. Vielhauer, "Gottesreich," 69.

19. Tödt, *Menschensohn,* 38. He quotes Rom. 1:16 and 2 Tim. 1:8.

PART THREE

The Kerygma of the
Earliest Church

3

THE CHURCH UNDER THE
LORDSHIP OF JESUS CHRIST

<hr />

The Christ Event: The Source of the
Church's Being

It seems fairly certain that Jesus was addressed by his disciples during his earthly ministry not only as "rabbi" but also as "*mar*" ("Lord"). (See, e.g., Mark 7:28; Matt. 7:21/Luke 6:46; John 13:13.) This, however, in the first instance could have meant no more than a purely honorific title such as was used in addressing any rabbi. No doubt as they came to see Jesus as the bearer of the decisive eschatological word of God, the acceptance or rejection of which determined their destiny in the coming kingdom of God, the term *mar* would begin to acquire a higher meaning. If the disciples began to entertain during the earthly life of Jesus the more specific hope that he himself was to perform the decisive act by which the kingdom of God should be actually inaugurated ("We had hoped that he was the one to redeem Israel"—Luke 24:21), the meaning of *mar* would have been even more elevated. But whatever degree of elevation it received must have been completely shattered by the crucifixion, when the disciples all forsook him and fled. It was the resurrection encounters which decisively transformed the meaning and content of *mar*.

Jesus as Lord

The risen Christ was still addressed by the disciples as *mar* (1 Cor. 16:22; cf. John 20:28), but it now meant what it had never meant before. The transformation is indicated by the fact that in Acts 2:26 *kyrios* (*mar*) is equated no longer with rabbi, but with *Christos,* anointed One. It definitely means that Jesus has been installed by God at his exaltation as the agent of redemption. Similarly in Phil. 2:9 the name *kyrios* is described as "the name which is above every name"; that is, the name of Yahweh himself (v. 11), as revealed to Israel in his mighty acts (Exod. 3:14) in the redemptive history of Israel. It is important to notice that both of these passages (Acts 2:36 and Phil. 2:9) insist that it is *God* who conferred on Jesus the status of *kyrios:* it is God who *made* Jesus Lord and Christ, and God who *gave* him the name above every name. The church's confession, *Iesous Kyrios,* Jesus is Lord, is not its own conferral of a status upon Jesus in its own estimation, springing perhaps from its own existential experience of the saving significance of the cross. The confession is rather the recognition of an already existing cosmic fact, over and above, though of course including, the existential experience of salvation in the cross.

The term used in the confession, *kyrios-mar,* is undoubtedly of human origin (there would in principle be no objection to calling it "mythological"). But over and above and behind the use of the term in the confession, there stands, not an existential experience alone, but an anterior act of God not merely upon the disciples, but upon Jesus. Nor is the confession "Jesus is Lord" a propositional dogma taught by Jesus and therefore repeated by believers as a *theologoumenon.* Neither is it a human assessment of Jesus' character as a man, or of the impact of his personality. It is a response to the revelation contained in the resurrection encounters in which God declared that he had acted eschatologically in Jesus. This does not of course mean that the earthly history of Jesus of Nazareth, and in particular his proclamation, has no relation whatever to the church's confession, that the confession springs as it were, exclusively from the resurrection, like Pallas Athene from the head of

Zeus. There *is* a relation between the proclamation of Jesus and the church's proclamation and confession. Jesus proclaimed: the reign of God has drawn nigh; God is beginning to act eschatologically (the implication, never explicitly uttered, it seems, being, "in me, in my words and works"). The resurrection however testifies that God's eschatological activity has advanced a stage further: God *has* now acted eschatologically in Jesus. Thus there can be no going back to the Jesus of history as such in order to correct the church's proclamation. But there must be a continual going back to the Jesus of history as seen in the light of the resurrection. This is what the Gospels do. For in the Jesus of history we see, in the light of the resurrection, God-having-acted eschatologically. We see what is meant by the confession "Jesus is Lord."

Translated by the earliest Greek-speaking communities from *mar* to *kyrios,* the confession "Jesus is Lord" was used antagonistically in opposition to the various *kyrios*-mythologies of the Greco-Roman world. It was used in opposition to the "lords many" of the Hellenistic-oriental mystery religions (1 Cor. 8:5). It was used in opposition to the imperial cult of *kyrios kaisar* (Mart. Polyc. viii). But it was never a question of transferring arbitrarily the content of belief from these alternative cult deities to Jesus. Jesus did not become a "cult deity." Normative Christian worship and prayer were never directed to the exalted Jesus as the end and term of that worship and prayer. Normative Christian worship and prayer were directed rather *to* the Father *through* the Son, in response to the Father's redemptive action in the Son. There are, of course, occasions in which prayer is apparently directed to the Son (e.g., Acts 7:59). But such occasions are strictly exceptional and "paraliturgical" in character.

Kyrios as the confession of God's act in Jesus has its primary reference to a constitutive past: God *has* acted eschatologically in the history of Jesus of Nazareth. But it has also important present and future references. Jesus was not only made Lord: He *is* Lord (Acts 10:36b). That is to say, God *continues* to act eschatologically in Jesus. "Jesus is Lord" is therefore also an affirmation about this present. Hence the frequent citations of Ps. 110:1 and the frequent statements, derived from that psalm, about Christ's session at the right hand of God (Acts 2:34, etc., no less than nineteen times in the NT). This means that the history of Jesus did not, as it were, deistically initiate the church's proclamation and set it in motion, so that the proclamation having once been inaugurated, God continues to act eschatologically upon the believers directly, without reference to the history of Jesus of Nazareth and his act in him. What God does through the church's proclamation is precisely to make his eschatological action in the past history of Jesus present and available. That also is part of what is meant by the confession "Jesus is Lord."

Again, the lordship of Christ has reference to the future. "He will come again." Both in the resurrection encounters themselves, which originated the *parousia*-hope, and in the continued encounters with God in Christ through the church's proclamation, there is a sense of incompleteness, of "not yet" (Rom. 8:23; Phil. 3:13; Heb. 2:8; 1 John 3:2), together with the assurance that this incompleteness will be made good by a consummation of that which is already given "in part" (1 Cor. 13:10). Thus Christ's exercise of his lordship is, in the perspective of the New Testament, temporally limited. It begins at his exaltation and lasts until the *parousia* (Acts 1:11 and 1 Cor. 15:24f.—note the "until" in v. 25). As we will see, this time of Christ's lordship coincides with the time of the church.

The Church as the Result of God's Redemptive Act in Christ

Did Jesus intend to found a church? The center and focal point of Jesus' proclamation was the reign of God, which is presented in apocalyptic terms, though with a considerable reduction of the apocalyptic imagery. This reign, in his perspective, was coming. It was not already realized, but though future, was already breaking through in advance of its actual coming. Since his whole emphasis was on the coming reign of God as such, there is no strong emphasis in his teaching that this involves a future eschatological community, though the idea is certainly there, e.g., Matt. 22:2ff. (*people* are to be summoned to the messianic banquet, cf. Luke 14:16ff.);

Matt. 8:11 para. (Q) (*many* shall be gathered at the end); Mark 12:26—God will reign among the "living"—that is to say, he will not reign in isolation from a resurrected people. This people will enjoy the privileges and prerogatives of Israel. This theme runs all through the Beatitudes (Matt. 5:3ff. para.). The people of the age to come will be called "sons of God" as Israel was. They shall "inherit the land" of the fulfilled kingdom as Israel inherited the promised land of Canaan after the exodus. The acceptance of Jesus' eschatological message as the sign of the coming reign of God is the sole factor which decides whether one will enter it or not, whether one will become a member of that people, whether one will be accepted by God (Matt. 11:6).

But Jesus not only announced the coming reign of God. He also declared himself just before his death to be about to accomplish the decisive act through which that reign should come. He declared himself to be about to die for the "many," in other words, to establish the eschatological community. Whether he conceived that community as one which would continue to exist in history in an interval between its inauguration and the final consummation is a matter which it is difficult to decide one way or the other. Some of the evidence points toward Jesus' catering for an interval between the cross and the *parousia,* while other evidence suggests a consummation supervening perhaps immediately upon his death. The question is ultimately immaterial, since it is cleared up by the resurrection encounters, which, as we have seen, revealed an interval between the "already" and the "not yet."

The disciples were not, then, during the earthly ministry of Jesus, a "church." But since Jesus was more than a rabbi, since he was the sign of the coming reign of God, so too the disciples were, in a somewhat different way, signs of the coming reign. The number twelve (for the historicity of this number, see the unimpeachable evidence of 1 Cor. 15:5), the inner core of the disciple band, shows that the disciples were the nucleus of the future eschatological community. The Qumran community, it is true, had a similar self-understanding. Yet there is a crucial difference, for since the eschatological proclamation of Jesus had begun, the disciples were nearer to the eschatological community than the

people of Qumran. Just as Jesus was the hidden Son of man designate (whether he was aware of it or not, a matter about which
New Testament scholars differ), so we may say that the disciples
were the hidden church designate. As Jesus of Nazareth is related
to the coming Son of man, so the disciples are related to the coming eschatological community. "The question whether Jesus made
his disciples into a church must be answered negatively. Yet the
idea of an ecclesia is deeply rooted in Jesus' work" (N.A. Dahl).

It is the resurrection which is decisive for the foundation of
the church, as it is for the lordship of Jesus. It is true that the famous
saying to Peter about the building of the church in Matt. 16:17–19
is represented as having been spoken by the historical Jesus, but this
saying probably belonged originally to the tradition of the "lost"
resurrection appearance to Peter. In any case, the saying goes back
to the earliest postresurrection community in Palestine. With the
first appearance to Peter, the foundation of the church is laid. Then
come the Twelve and then the five hundred (1 Cor. 15:5f.). Then,
after the foundation members, come those who believe through the
apostle's word. The word *ekklesia* (Heb. *qahal,* Aramaic *qehala*) thus
originates in the self-understanding of the earliest Christian community, which believed itself to be constituted by Jesus' death and
resurrection as the eschatological people of God.

Traditionally, Pentecost has been regarded as the "birthday"
of the Christian church. This is erroneous insofar as it is based on
the late, artificial chronology of Acts 1–2, with its serialization of
the resurrection, forty days' appearances, ascension, ten days' waiting, and the outpouring of the Spirit finally at Pentecost. There is,
however, an element of truth in the tradition insofar as the church is
the outcome of the total complex, the death-resurrection-exaltation
of Jesus and the consequent gift of the Spirit. Thus the lordship of
Christ and the existence of the church belong inseparably together.

The Church and Grace

It is significant that the church calls itself *qahal* (*qehala*), and not
ʾedhah. Both words mean the assembled people of God. But ʾedhah

had come to mean the people of the synagogue, meticulously obeying the law and waiting for the decisive eschatological intervention of God in the future. *Qahal,* on the other hand, had come to be restricted to the earliest days of the people of God just after the exodus, while it was still in the wilderness, while it was still conscious of the intervention of God which had made them his people in its immediate past. The early Christian community had the same vivid consciousness of the intervention of God immediately behind them. *Qahal* thus means a community which is oriented primarily toward its immediate past and its present (though of course a future orientation is not entirely excluded, as witness the hope of entry into Canaan: the hope however is qualified decisively by the past and present). In this connection it is perhaps particularly significant that the Qumran community, for all its eschatological selfconsciousness, never, so far as the documents hitherto discovered indicate, called itself *qahal,* but only *'edhah.* Qumran was still looking forward to the decisive eschatological intervention in the future. The Christian community knew that this intervention was already behind them. Jesus *is* Lord. The reign of God has been inaugurated, even though it still awaits consummation in the future, and even though the church is still to that extent a waiting community. It is not, however, waiting for something new, but only for the consummation of the salvation which it already enjoys, the manifestation of that which is already there but hidden. This is the difference between the future orientation of the *qahal* and that of the *'edhah.*

The Nature of the Church's Being

It is, as we have seen, the act of God in Christ which established the church. For those who were in immediate contact with that event, for those who had consorted with Jesus from Galilee to Jerusalem, were witnesses of his resurrection appearances and had received the Spirit directly from him (Peter, the Twelve, the five hundred, and also—if they are not included in the five hundred—the women who had ministered to Jesus and his mother and brethren). That was all that was necessary to bring them into the *ekklesia.* These together form the foundation members of the church. Others have to be brought into relation with the redemptive event by the kerygma, that is to say, the proclamation of the redemptive event by its witnesses, or in the case of those who in space or time are out of the immediate range of the apostolic witness, by those who are derivative from and dependent upon that witness.

The Reception of the Gospel

The kerygma, for all its manifold forms of expression, contains two inalienable elements: the report of certain concrete historical happenings involving the man Jesus of Nazareth; and the proclamation that in and through these happenings God had acted eschatologically. But the announcement and acceptance of the proclamation is not in itself sufficient to establish direct contact with the redemptive event. This direct contact is established by baptism. For baptism is the equivalent for those that come after to the direct participation which the original disciples had with the redemptive event. It is their "total immersion" in the event, their transference into that eschatological existence which the event made possible. Without baptism, the kerygma would be simply a past event reported with an accompanying interpretation as the redemptive act of God. But the event needs not only to be reported and interpreted; it needs to become a present reality for participation, and this is something that God alone can do. Without baptism the kerygma becomes something merely talked about, not something in which men may participate here and now. In and through the human action of baptism, however, God takes his redemptive act in Christ out of the past and makes it a present event for participation. Baptism is thus an act in which the lordship of Jesus Christ becomes effectively operative as a present reality. It is significant that the Acts of the Apostles speaks of those who are brought into the church by the apostolic preaching and baptism as "being added" to the church (Acts 2:41, 47; 5:14; 11:24). This phraseology enshrines two important conceptions. First, the passive verb "were added" is a "reverential passive," the agent of which is God himself, as is made clear in 2:47, where it is directly stated that it is "the Lord" (i.e., God acting eschatologically in Christ) who added the converts to the church. Second, the church is the already existing apostolic community prior to the entry of those added. For the church is not a voluntary association of those who have already become believers in individual isolation. To think otherwise would be to deny the lordship of Christ over the church.

But the church is not an assured possession or an established institution. Its being as church has constantly to be renewed. It has to continue "in the apostles' teaching and fellowship, in the breaking of the bread." There is a continuing ministry of the apostolic word in the church, a renewal of the original kerygma, which the New Testament calls *paraklesis* (Heb. 13:22). Once again, however, it is not enough simply to talk about the Christ event. This event must become by God's action a renewed reality in the midst of the congregation. That is what happens in the breaking of the bread. Like baptism, this is an action of the church ("Do this," *this* referring not only to the eating of the bread and drinking of the cup, but to the total action, taking the bread, giving thanks, breaking, and receiving). But this action of the church, just as in baptism, is met and crossed by the action of God which makes present his redemptive act in Christ. This is the meaning of the promise "This is my body. . . . This is my blood." Body and blood here denote not "substances" but event—the event of God's redemptive act in Christ. We might speak of "transeventualization" rather than "transubstantiation" as being what happens in the eucharist. In any case, the eucharist is a real manifestation of the lordship of Christ. *Marana tha* (1 Cor. 16:22) is not so much a prayer for the second coming, but a prayer that Christ should come in the eucharist as a renewal of his coming in his death-resurrection and as an anticipation of his coming in the *parousia*.

The Church's Obedience to Christ's Mission

Christ is the supreme *apostolos* of God (Heb. 3:1), the one sent by the Father (Mark 9:37b para.; John 4:34, and frequently). His sending was not incidental or peripheral to his other activities, but was the ground and basis of them all. His sending embraced all that he was and said and did.

His mission accomplished, he sends others to continue his mission (John 20:21; 1 Cor. 1:17; cf. Matt. 28:19–20). The sending of the church likewise is not incidental or peripheral to its other activities, but is the ground and basis of them all. Its sending embraces all that it is and says and does. In the words of the contemporary cliché, the church *is* mission; it does not have, *inter alia,* a mission. That mission is to prolong and continue the mission of the Son. As Jesus by his human obedience provided the occasion in and through which God wrought his mighty act of redemption, so the church, by her obedience, provides the occasion through which God continues and renews his act of redemption. Thus mission and Christ's lordship go together. In the manifold activities which embrace her mission the church manifests the lordship of Christ. She witnesses, as we have already seen, in the kerygma. She witnesses in the obedient performance of baptism. She witnesses in the *paraklesis,* the continued preaching of the Word of God in the congregation. She witnesses when she assembles for the breaking of the bread. But there are other ways in which she witnesses, which we have not yet mentioned: she witnesses by the agape which she shows to them that are without. She witnesses too by suffering for the gospel's sake at the hands of an unbelieving and hostile world. Thus the church's witness to the lordship of Christ has to be both kerygmatic and existential, both by her spoken word and rites, and also by the quality of the life she lives. It is neither of these without the other.

The Function of the Church

"The church is not only the community which proclaims God's acts to the world, but also the community which appropriates and enjoys the new life in Christ, which walks in his ways, and which praises God for his deeds."

"Which Proclaims God's Acts to the World"

First, the church enjoys the new life in Christ. It is important to note both the reality and the preliminary character of this new life. On the one hand, it is not merely a fictitious pronouncing righteous of sinners who remain in themselves sinners all along and nothing more. It is not a merely external imputation of Christ's righteousness to the believers who remain unaffected in their sin. The love of God *has* been shed abroad in our hearts (Rom. 5:1ff.). We *are* sons of God in the Son (Romans 8). We are "in Christ"— that is, we really participate in his eschatological existence. For the Johannine author, life in the church is a rebirth (John 3) and a new life in which we abide in Christ and he in us (John 15). God's word of justification, by which we are pronounced righteous for Christ's sake, has also the power to make us righteous, for God's word is creative: it has the power to accomplish what it says. Yet the Christian believer and the church itself always remain *in via*. Believers are always sinners, though they have been accepted by God by the forgiveness of sins and given the power to become what they are— saints. Thus the renewed being has to be constantly renewed by penitence, by the hearing of the word of forgiveness, by the receiving of the sacrament. The church, therefore, is summoned to testify to the lordship of Christ by walking in his ways. The ethical demand is inseparable from the Christian gospel.

It is important, however, to define aright the place of ethical behavior in the Christian scheme. It has not the same place as the works of the law in Judaism. The works of the law were done in prospect of a decisive eschatological event which was yet to come in the future. Indeed, they were done to bring about that event, or at least to accelerate it. If all Israel kept one sabbath perfectly, the kingdom of God would come! For the Christian *ekklesia,* however, the decisive event has already occurred, and therefore in no sense can good works have the purpose of bringing it about or accelerating it. Therefore, to seek justification by the works of the law is to deny that the eschatological event has taken place (Gal. 2:21b). Yet when the eschatological event is already behind us, we still stand under the divine imperative, for the imperative is now undertaken, not in order to bring about the eschatological event, but because that event has already been brought about and because obedience is the response which it requires. Moreover, it is a response which is created by the eschatological event itself, where that is accepted in faith (cf. the Pauline notion of the "fruit of the Spirit").

"We were buried therefore with him by baptism into death, so that as Christ was raised from the dead by the glory of the Father, we too might walk in newness of life" (Rom. 6:4). Here Paul asserts that the same eschatological energy of God which raised Jesus from the dead works to produce obedience in the believers. "If you then have been raised with Christ, seek those things that are above, where Christ is seated at the right hand of God" (Col. 3:1). Here Paul asserts that although Christian obedience is from one point of view produced by the eschatological activity of God, from another perspective it demands concentrated human effort. This is a paradox: "Work out your own salvation with fear and trembling; for God is at work in you" (Phil. 2:12f.). "I live; and yet no longer I, but Christ liveth in me" (Gal. 2:20, ERV; RSV misses the paradox). But the paradox is the same as that of Jesus of Nazareth himself. On the one hand his history is the humble offering of perfect human obedience; on the other it is the eschatological act of God. "In this is love, not that we loved God, but that he loved us and sent his Son to be the expiation for our sins. Beloved, if God so loved us, we ought also to love one another" (1 John 4:10f.). In this passage the Johannine author emphasizes the character of the Christian's ethical life as response. Thus the ground and basis of the Christian ethic is the fact of Christ's lordship, that is, the fact that in him God performed the decisive act of redemption. The Christian ethic is a manifestation of the lordship of Christ.

"Which Appropriates and Enjoys the New Life in Christ"

The content of the Christian ethic is, of course, agape: "Thou shalt love the Lord thy God . . . and thy neighbor as thyself." First then, it is to love God. But we must be careful there. For, "in this is love, not that we love God, but that he loved us." Our love for God is never something which we ourselves initiate, but always a love which is related to his initiation. Our love to God rests exclusively upon our being loved by him. Nor can our love for him be in any sense an independent response on our part, chronologically secondary to, yet ontologically distinct from it. To love God means to let him perform his redemptive action upon you, to let Christ be Lord to you. In other words, love of God means *faith*.

The Christian's love of his neighbor must likewise be distinguished from all merely human service to him, though human service may often be involved. For even "if I bestow all my goods to feed the poor, but have not love, it profiteth me nothing" (1 Cor. 13:3). To do service uninformed by Christian love means to love apart from God's love in Christ. Christian love is not only chronologically secondary to God's love for us in Christ, as though that love were something independent of and external to God's love in Christ. Christian love is ontologically continuous with God's love in Christ, partakes of the same quality, and is of one essence with it. Now God's love for us in Christ is essentially love concretely exhibited in the act of forgiveness: "God shows his love for us in that while we were yet sinners Christ died for us" (Rom. 5:8).

The whole ministry of Jesus was an actualization of this divine love for sinners, as when he ate and drank with publicans and sinners, and when he interpreted this action by the parables of the lost (Luke 15). This ministry culminated in the cross, interpreted at the last supper as the giving of his life as a ransom for many, enacted parabolically in the giving of the bread and wine to his disciples. So too the love of Christians toward others is supremely activated in forgiveness: "Love your enemies and pray for those who persecute you . . . so that you may be sons of your Father who is in heaven; for he makes his sun to rise on the evil and on the good, and sends rain on the just and on the unjust" (Matt. 5:45). "Forgiving one another, as God in Christ forgave you" (Eph. 4:32). Here, in forgiveness, lies the distinctively Christian feature of the Christian ethic. Formally and externally, the content of the Christian ethic is so often disappointing; it looks like nothing more than a rehash of rabbinic or Stoic ethics. This is perfectly true, but the rabbinic and Stoic ethics are transformed by the spirit of forgiveness. Thereby Christian behavior becomes witness to the lordship of Christ (cf. the "*en kyrio*" which Paul inserts into the household codes; Col. 3:18ff.).

"Which Walks in His Ways"

The world may reject both the word of proclamation and the loving service of the church. The church has then no alternative but to suffer at the hands of a godless world (Mark 13:11ff.; Matt. 10:16ff.; John 15:18ff.). This is perhaps the most powerful witness the church can give to the lordship of Christ. The blood of the martyrs in the Apocalypse is the most potent ingredient the church can offer to the final victory of Christ as "King of kings and Lord of lords." But in persecution and martyrdom, the culmination of true discipleship, there is no room for mock heroics. The church can only pray, "lead us not into temptation" (*peirasmos,* the temptation to abandon faith in the lordship of Christ in the supreme hour of trial). She can only pray that she may be given grace, having done all, to stand.

"Which Praises God for His Deeds"

We have placed this element last, though it is the focal point of everything that has been already said. For it is in the liturgy that the church expresses what she is in her inmost being. It is in her liturgy that she manifests the lordship of Christ. It is not for nothing that the confession of Christ as Lord first took place in a liturgical context (*Marana tha*).

Liturgy does not mean fixed prayers read out of a book. Liturgy is not the accidental preliminary to or framework of preaching. Liturgy is the obedient action of the church in response to the redemptive action of God in Christ. It is her grateful confession of Christ's lordship. Liturgy is the recitation and rehearsal before God of his mighty acts whereby he has constituted the church as his people. It is the Godward action of the whole priestly body. "Through him then let us offer up a sacrifice to God, that is, the fruit of lips that acknowledge his name" (Heb. 13:15). "A holy priesthood, to offer up spiritual sacrifices acceptable to God through Jesus Christ" (1 Pet. 2:5). "But you are a chosen race, a royal priesthood, a holy nation, God's own people, that you may declare (i.e., recite before him in liturgy) the wonderful deeds of him who called you out of darkness into his own marvelous light" (1 Peter 2:9). The church's liturgy, as the rehearsal of God's mighty acts which constitute her being, has its roots in the old covenant. (See, e.g., such liturgical recitations as Deut. 26:5ff.; 1 Kings 8:14ff., and the blessings, *berakoth,* of later Judaism.) The early church understood Jesus at the last supper to have replaced the liturgy of the old covenant, with its rehearsal of the mighty acts of God in the exodus which constituted old Israel as his people, by a new liturgy, which should rehearse God's eschatological redemption performed in him: "Do this in remembrance of *me.*" Like the Old Testament recitations of God's mighty acts, and like the late Jewish *berakoth,* this remembrance before God of his mighty act in Christ calls forth the action of God which makes his mighty act in the past present here and now. In this way the church is renewed in her existence as the people of God. Thus it is in the liturgy that the lordship of Christ is manifested. That is why Sunday is the *Lord's* day (Rev. 1:10).

The Local Church and the Church Universal

A cursory reading of the New Testament gives the impression that the word "church" (*ekklesia*) was used with primary reference to the local congregation and that the notion of the universal church was achieved by adding up the local congregations. It is true that the term *ekklesia* was first used of itself by the local congregation at Jerusalem. It is true also that, as the gospel spread, *ekklesia* was used of other local congregations, as at Antioch (Acts 11:26, etc.) and Ephesus (20:17), and cf. the Pauline epistles. Then as the churches multiply, we find the word used of the whole church (Acts 9:31; 20:28). But to conceive the development thus is to overlook the Old Testament roots of the word. *Ekklesia* means the people of God established by his eschatological act in Christ, as it had meant the people of God established by the exodus. There can be only one eschatological people of God, though this one people is susceptible of local manifestations or embodiments (not denominational embodiments, as we are prone to think today, for that is a complete travesty of the New Testament perspective).

4

THE RESURRECTION OF
JESUS CHRIST

"The resurrection itself is not an event of past history. All that historical criticism can establish is the fact that the first disciples came to believe in the resurrection" (R. Bultmann in "New Testament and Mythology," Kerygma and Myth, *p. 42).*

"The resurrection of Christ cannot be an objective fact of history in the same sense as was the crucifixion of Jesus. . . . That is an area where the historian cannot operate" (G. Ernest Wright in The Book of the Acts of God, *p. 25).*

The Resurrection: Faith Event or Historical Fact?

There are two main schools of thought on the subject of the resurrection. There are those who stoutly maintain that the resurrection is a "historical" fact, and that on this historicity the whole Christian faith depends. There are those who, while they would agree that the whole Christian faith depends on belief in the resurrection, nevertheless are at pains to deny that the resurrection is in the ordinary sense of the word a historical fact. By this they mean that it is not a datum with which the historian can operate. Why is this so? There are two reasons. First, as G. Ernest Wright has indicated in the sequel to the passage which heads this chapter, "the crucifixion was a fact available to all men as a real happening, and pagan writers like Tacitus and Josephus can speak about it. But in the New Testament itself the Easter faith event is perceived only by the people of faith. Christ as risen was not seen by everyone, but only by the few." Of course, this circumstance does not in itself make the resurrection a nonhistorical event in the ordinary sense of the word. Julius Caesar's birth was presumably witnessed only by the few people directly concerned—the mother, the father possibly, the midwife, and the household slaves—yet no one would deny its historicity in the ordinary sense of the word. The paucity of witnesses does not of itself place an event beyond the historian's ken. There is a second and more potent reason for this, the reason which Wright alludes to when he says that Christ as risen was perceptible only to the people of faith.

Richard R. Niebuhr, in his book *Revelation and Historical Reason,* has criticized the application of modern historical method to the understanding of the resurrection. His thesis is that this is to impose alien categories upon biblical thought, whereas the biblical concept of history as the area of God's working is *sui generis,* and, if we are to understand the Bible, this concept must be taken as it stands. The exegete's task is to listen to the kerygma and let it speak for itself, with all its strangeness to our modern conceptions of historicity. One possible objection to Niebuhr's position would be to take Bultmann's line and ask whether by a *sacrificium intellectus* a person must first accept the biblical view of history, which is so opposed to his own, before he can accept the kerygma? We hear Bultmann protesting that this is to confront a person with an inauthentic *scandalon,* and to make it impossible for him to face up to the authentic *scandalon* of the kerygma itself; that it is to deprive faith of its character of pure decision, and to reduce it to the status of a work. After all, it is our destiny as people of the twentieth century to accept the modern, scientific attitude to history.

Such a criticism would have its point, were it not for the fact that the biblical view of history itself presents us with just the kind of distinction between empirical occurrence and faith event the proponents of the *Heilsgeschichte* interpretation advance. For the

Bible itself distinguishes between observable occurrence and faith interpretation in the case of revelatory events. The observable occurrence is always open to a nonfaith interpretation. A clear example of this is the exorcisms of Jesus. In themselves they are part of the observable flux of history; they may be "miraculous," but then other historical events may be equally so. The sons of the Pharisees also cast out demons. It is not in their observable "miraculous" character that their revelatory significance lies. That significance cannot be "read off" from Jesus' exorcisms. As events of observable history, however, they are susceptible of varying interpretations. One may say, it is by Beelzebul that Jesus casts out demons (Luke 11:15). On the other hand, one may see in them the activity of the "finger of God" ushering in his eschatological rule (Luke 11:20), in other words, that the occurrences in question are revelatory and faith events. The same holds good of the total Christ event. It is possible to say, from the standpoint of nonfaith, *"anathema Iesous"* (1 Cor. 12:3). But by revelation responded to by faith ("by the Holy Spirit") one may say *"Kyrios Iesous."* If the faith interpretation resided observably in the occurrence itself, there would be no need of prophetic (i.e., Old Testament) and apostolic (i.e., New Testament) witness of the acts of God in history. The biblical faith events therefore contain two facets: the observable historical occurrence which is in principle capable of historical verification by all the methods of modern scientific historical methodology; and the revelatory significance, the establishment of which is beyond the province of the scientific historian and is accessible only to faith. In asserting this, we are not simply conceding what the present-day historian, as opposed to his nineteenth-century predecessor, is prepared to concede, namely, that it is impossible to write "objective" history, since every historian inevitably and rightly interprets history in the light of his own presuppositions. We are not dealing here with "presuppositions" imposed upon the biblical history by the writers of that history, or with human "interpretations." We are dealing rather with "revelation," which precisely *shatters* all human presuppositions and interpretations. Confronted by Good Friday, the historian can only say with the disciples on the road to Emmaus, "We had hoped that he was the one to redeem Israel" (Luke 24:21).

Niebuhr's protest against certain kinds of *heilsgeschichtlich* interpretations, in which the past-historical occurrences which revelation and faith interpret are either denied to have happened at all, or are reduced to shadowy unimportance, is wholly justified. This is the danger of what N. A. Dahl has aptly called "kerygmatic docetism."[1] In the biblical witness both facets are invariably found: the past-historical occurrence and the revelatory interpretation. The first element must be explored with the tools of modern scientific historical criticism. The second element is the material which the New Testament *theologian* has to expound. We will follow these two processes in turn with the New Testament witness to the resurrection of Jesus.

The Historical Character of the Resurrection

The earliest statement about the resurrection, as is generally acknowledged, is in Paul's quotation of a kerygmatic formula in 1 Cor. 15:3–7. E. Bammel has subjected this passage to an analysis with the methods of *Traditionsgeschichte*.[2] As a result he discovers the passage to be composite, consisting of three originally distinct formulae, which he numbers formulae I, II, and III respectively. Formula I is a four-line verse:

> *Christos apethanen hyper ton hamartion hēmon kata tas graphas*
> *kai etaphē*
> *kai egēgertai tē hēmera tē tritē kata tas graphas*
> *kai ophthē*

There is the same number of words in each line, rhyme ending, and a combination of synthetic and antithetic parallelism, all features of Semitic poetry. There are other features pointing to the earliest Palestinian church as the *Sitz im Leben* of the formula: (1) the anarthrous *Christos,* a Hebraism as in John 4:25 (*oida hoti messias erchetai*) and Dan. 9:25 (*'adh mashiah*); (2) the *hyper* theology, characteristic of the earliest Palestinian church, and distinctively non-Pauline, except where Paul is quoting traditional formulae;[3] (3) the reverential passive *egēgertai* and the use of *ophthē* instead of *ephanē*, representing Hebrew *nirʾah*.[4] We note here that the first two verbs *apethanen* and *etaphē* refer to historical occurrences, that is, occurrences which are in principle open to historical verification. The *egēgertai* and *ophthē* are however faith events; that is to say, they contain within themselves two elements, an implied historical occurrence, capable in principle of historical verification, and an explicit faith interpretation, that is, the interpretation of the implied past-historical occurrence as an act of God. Let us examine each in turn.

Egēgertai

It has become almost an axiom of critical orthodoxy that the occurrence of which this faith assertion is the believing interpretation is the post-Easter visions of the disciples. The writer must confess that he shared this view when he began to work on this chapter. Further study of the resurrection pericopes, however, suggests that the visions are never presented as the occasion of the revelation that "God has raised Jesus." In the vision pericopes his having been raised is invariably assumed. Rather, the disconcerting fact emerges that the revelation of the fact that God raised Jesus is asserted in connection with the visit of the women to the tomb (cf. Mark 16:6, *egērthē*, which is the revelatory interpretation of the visible fact, *ouk estin hode*.) I am aware, of course, of all the critical difficulties attaching to this pericope, as indicated by Lohmeyer *ad loc*. Mark 16:1 makes a fresh start with a new list of names of the women, after 15:40 and 47. The passion narrative points forward to an appearance only (14:28), not to the empty tomb. Mark 16:7 is clearly an editorial insertion modeled on 14:28 to effect a juncture between the newly inserted pericope and the preceding passion narrative: when v. 7 is removed, v. 8 follows more intelligibly upon v. 6, and the contradiction between vv. 7 and 8 is removed. Yet these same facts all indicate that the whole pericope is pre-Markan. Mark was trying to fit together two different traditions he found in the material at his disposal. The empty tomb was not part of the original passion narrative, just as it was not part of the kerygma (1 Cor. 15:4). What then was its *Sitz im Leben?* It is commonly regarded as an apologetic legend designed to answer the charges that the disciples stole the body or as an attempt to prove to doubters the reality of the resurrection. These, however, are post-Markan motives, the former appearing only in Matthew (the bribing of the guard), the latter in Luke and John (male witnesses as well as women, who were not qualified to give evidence). The *Sitz im Leben* is neither apology nor proof.[5] Nevertheless the pericope has a close connection with the kerygma. It culminates in the angelic pronouncement, *egērthē* (the almost exact equivalent of the kerygmatic *egēgertai* in 1 Cor. 15:4), *ouk estin hode.* I suggest therefore that the *Sitz im Leben* of the empty tomb pericope is the postkerygmatic didache explaining to neophytes how it was that the kerygma asserted that God had raised Jesus, what historical occurrence it was that the revelational and faith assertion, *egēgertai (egērthē)*, was intended to interpret. That historical occurrence was the *ouk estin hode,* the body was not in the tomb. All the kerygmatic assertions, even the earliest one in 1 Cor. 15:3ff., must therefore be taken to *imply* the empty tomb, even though they do not directly assert it. There is corroborative evidence that this is so in 1 Corinthians 15. The presence of *etaphē* and *tē tritē hēmera* point in the same direction. The whole argumentation of 1 Cor. 15:20 presupposes a bodily resurrection, as does the baptismal symbolism of Romans 6. Indeed, it is hard to see what sense any Jew could attach to *egēgertai* apart from *bodily* resurrection. We therefore reject the contention of those critics who deny that Paul or the pre-Pauline tradition knew of the empty tomb. This—and not the appearances—is the historical occurrence which the resurrection faith interprets.

Two notes of warning are in order here. First, we have not proven the historicity of the empty tomb. We have only endeavored to demonstrate that it belongs to the earliest kerygmatic tradition. Further back than this we can only discuss probabilities. All we can say is that the faith assertion was never, so far as our evidence goes, regarded as interpretative of any other past-historical occurrence. Second, even if the historicity of the empty tomb were susceptible of certain proof, it would still not be a proof of the resurrection faith. We would still have only an empty tomb, only the past historical occurrence of the *ouk estin hode,* which would be susceptible of other, and unbelieving, interpretations. Either Jewish contention that the body was stolen or removed, or the rationalist suggestion that the women went to the wrong tomb, would be viable alternatives. We know that God raised Christ from the dead only through the preaching of the church and the response of faith. That is why the assertion *egērthē* is made, not as direct historical narration, but as the report of an angel—it is suprahistorical revelation.

Ōphthē

But the kerygmatic tradition further asserts that Christ appeared. This statement again contains two facets—the past-historical fact that the disciples underwent certain experiences, the historicity of which even Bultmann assumes when he speaks of the *Ostererlebnisse* of the disciples, and which is necessary to account for the rise of the kerygma after Good Friday, and the faith interpretation that these were really appearances, that is to say, revelations of the risen Christ vouchsafed by God. Once again, as in the case of *egēgertai,* so in the case of *ophthē,* we are posed with a twofold problem: first, to trace back as far as we can the tradition about the historical occurrence and to expose it in its earliest reachable form; and second, to explore the theological content of the suprahistorical revelation which the recipients believed themselves to have received in and through the past-historical occurrences.

We turn therefore to the historical problem. In 1 Cor. 15:3–8, Bammel discovers two further formulae:

Formula II: three appearances,	(1) to Peter
	(2) to the Twelve
	(3) to more than 500 brethren
Formula III: two appearances,	(1) to James
	(2) to all the apostles

Bammel suggests that these two formulae represent alternative traditions, rather than five consecutive appearances, the pattern in each formula being an extension from appearances to an individual to appearances to groups. The second appearance in each tradition (to the Twelve and to all the apostles) is the same occurrence. The third appearance to the five hundred or more has disappeared in the second tradition. The tradition of a primary appearance to James, Bammel suggests, represents a substitution for that to Peter, originating at the time when James took over the leadership of the Jerusalem community from Peter on the latter's departure ca. A.D. 42. That James was in fact the recipient of an appearance is a necessary postulate, since during the earthly life of Jesus he was not a disciple, but apparently a skeptical critic (Mark 3:21, 32–35), yet in Acts 1:14 he is included among the body of disciples. Bammel suggests that he was originally included among the five hundred brethren. It may, however, be better to assume that the Lord's family were recipients of a special appearance (or appearances) prior to the appearance to the five hundred, but that these were not included in the earlier formula because they had no foundational significance for the church. So we may fall back on Formula II as giving the earlier tradition.

First, the primary appearance to Peter. It is one of the curiosities of the New Testament that the Gospels contain no direct narrative of this appearance. But there are a number of traces of it. Mark 16:7 ("Go, tell his disciples and Peter") suggests that Mark knew of an appearance to Peter as well as to the Twelve, though the order is curious. It is alluded to in Luke 24:34 in almost identical wording with Formula II (*ophthē Simoni*). Luke 22:31 is probably also an allusion to the same occurrence ("when you have turned again, strengthen your brethren"). Then there is a much developed form of it in John 21:15–19, though its derivation from the primary appearance is fairly clear because, like all the traditions of the appearance to the Twelve, it represents Peter's commissioning to the apostolate. There are four other pericopes, all of which are now located in the earthly life of Jesus, but which, it has been claimed, are all derived from the primary postresurrection appearance to Peter. These are (1) Peter's confession at Caesarea Philippi (Mark

8:27ff.), (2) the transfiguration (Mark 9:1ff. and parallels), (3) the call of Peter after the miraculous draft of fishes (Luke 5:1ff.), (4) the *tu es Petrus* insertion by Matthew into the Markan pericope (Matt. 16:17–20). For various reasons I am not disposed to follow Bultmann[6] in relegating the first two of these in the category of misplaced resurrection appearances; but the case for the last two is much stronger. The Lukan call of Peter contains a number of features more appropriate to a postresurrection situation. Peter's words "Depart from me, for I am a sinful man, O Lord" (Luke 5:8) are more specific if they are a confession of his denial in the passion narrative. The emphasis on wonder (*thambos*, v. 9) and fear (*mē phobou*, v. 10) is a common feature in these appearances (e.g., Luke 24:37). The commission "henceforth you will be catching men" is better understood as Peter's commissioning to the apostolate, like the Johannine command to feed the sheep. And the miraculous draft of fishes appears in a postresurrection context in John 21.

Matthew 16:17ff. is a torso inserted into and interrupting the flow of the Markan dialogue at Caesarea Philippi. Yet its Palestinian coloring is admitted even by Bultmann.[7] If authentic, the only plausible situation for it, as Stauffer maintains,[8] is postresurrectional. Here again, the significance of the call to Peter is his institution to the primacy among the apostles. It is quite possible that Mark knew of this tradition and is alluding to it in Mark 16:7.

The appearance to the Twelve has survived firmly in the tradition, though in a number of variant forms. It is alluded to in Mark 16:7 and narrated in Matt. 28:16ff., Luke 24:26ff. and John 20:19–23. The common element is that the risen Lord commissions the Twelve to the apostolate.

All traces of the appearance to the five hundred brethren and more have disappeared from the gospel tradition, as is already the case with Formula III in 1 Corinthians 15. It has often been identified with the Pentecost even in Acts 2, in which, we infer from Acts 2, there were one hundred and twenty participants. This is possible, since the earliest church did not distinguish between the resurrection and ascension as separate moments (e.g., the appearance to Paul on the Damascus road, which the apostle classes among the other appearances in all respects save its lateness [*ektroma*], was an appearance of the risen and ascended Lord[9]). Moreover, John 20:10ff. shows that the gift of the Spirit is not confined in principle, as Luke suggests, to the Pentecost event, but was regarded as the direct impartation of the risen Christ at his appearances.

We conclude therefore that the three foundational postresurrection appearances in Bammel's Formula II are discernible in other parts of the tradition in the Gospels and Acts, that the tradition regards them as encounters with the risen and exalted One, and that he appears (1) in order to commission, first Peter, then the Twelve, then the foundation members of the church, to bear witness to God's saving act in him, and (2) in order to empower the apostles and the church with his Spirit for the execution of his commission.

The Theological Significance of the Resurrection

This brings us to the final aspect of our subject—the significance of *ophthē* for faith. What did the postresurrection encounter reveal to the participants? Here we are dealing, not with historical occurrences, but with the revelation which the occurrences contained for faith. Nor need we suppose or insist that the insights thus vouchsafed were conveyed directly and immediately through the occurrences, as the appearance pericopes tend to imply. As a matter of history, these insights may in some cases have come as a result of reflection upon the impact of the occurrences. But in either case, it is the occurrences, the resurrection encounters, which create the insights.

That the resurrection encounters were constitutive for faith is widely recognized today. To many (e.g., John Knox in his various writings), the Easter revelation offers a welcome escape from historical skepticism about Jesus of Nazareth. Many aspects of the life and teaching of the New Testament church, which since the time of the evangelist have derived their sanction from the supposedly historical logia of Jesus, can now be relegated to the church's experience of the risen Christ. Since their revelatory character is still maintained, it is possible to combine historical skepticism with credal orthodoxy. The writer must confess his sympathy with this approach. The resurrection *is* constitutive for the church's faith, and as we will see, for every aspect of that faith. We would agree with Barth's compliment to Bultmann: "One must give Bultmann credit for bringing to light and emphasizing the central, indispensable function of the Easter event for the thought and language of the New Testament."[10] The resurrection encounters are not just one of a chain of factors which gave rise to the affirmations and practices of the earliest church, but the constitutive factor.

It is also true that the Gospels have read back into the lifetime of Jesus much of its postresurrection faith, a circumstance which is particularly obvious in the transformation of resurrection appearances into scenes within the earthly life of Jesus. But it is possible to overstate this case in such a way as to lead to "kerygmatic docetism." It is a procedure reminiscent of the ancient gnostic thesis of a tradition derived from the Great Forty Days, and of Catholic modernism, which finds the authority for faith in the religious experience of the church, rather than in a revelation given in history. Moreover, a thoroughly critical approach to the history of Jesus need not result in such excessive skepticism as is usually displayed by the neo-orthodox. To sift out the postresurrection accretions to the traditions of the words and deeds of Jesus is a delicate procedure, but it is not impossible. The clue for our guidance is the difference of situation between Jesus and the early church. Jesus' activity was precross and preresurrection, and therefore prior to God's decisive eschatological act; the early church is postcross and postresurrection, and therefore subsequent to God's decisive eschatological act. Jesus had an understanding of his own history, but it is different from the early church's understanding of that same history in the light of the resurrection. Yet there is a continuous frame of reference between the two understandings. For Jesus, God was beginning his eschatological action and about to consummate it; for the early church, God had decisively accomplished that eschatological action and was shortly to consummate it. Once this is seen, it is possible to retain the legitimate concern of neo-orthodoxy for the decisive importance of the resurrection faith, without lapsing into kerygmatic docetism or driving so deep a wedge between Jesus and the church as to make their continuity unintelligible. We will find that while the resurrection contains real revelation, this revelation is not a bolt from the blue, given entirely *de novo,* but is foreshadowed in genuine historical elements in the life of Jesus, albeit, in the form of prophecy and promise. As we examine the facets of the Easter revelation, we will find that in each case, while there is real revelation, the revelation has its roots in the Jesus of history.

It was the resurrection appearances which revealed to the disciples that the whole preceding history of Jesus—his life, ministry, death, and resurrection, and the empty tomb—were in fact the eschatological act of God. At the same time there was a genuine historical relationship between the eschatology of Jesus and that of the early church. In the risen Lord's self-proclamation to the Twelve in Matt. 28:16ff. there is a direct allusion to the vision of the coming kingdom in Daniel 7. In Acts 1:3, 6–8 the risen Lord is represented as discussing with the disciples the subject of the kingdom in terms which imply that the gift of the Spirit is a real installment in the coming of the kingdom. The meals of the risen Lord with the disciples (Luke 24:30, 41; John 21:9ff; Acts 1:4 [*synalizomenos*], 10:41) are clearly meant to be in some partial sense, at any rate, fulfillments of the eschatological predictions in Mark 14:25, Luke 22:16, 30. Now it is universally agreed that Jesus spoke of the kingdom of God in his teaching, though scholars are not agreed as to whether he spoke of it as having already come or as imminent. If we take the view that in his ministry Jesus regarded it as imminent and dawning, but not yet come, then we have both continuity and difference in the Easter revelation. By it the disciples are brought to see that through the cross and resurrection the second phase in the eschatological process has arrived; whereas before Good Friday the kingdom had been dawning, it is now decisively inaugurated.

It is clear that the Easter revelation was constitutive for the primitive Christology. The so-called adoptionist formulae of the earliest strata of the New Testament indicate that Jesus was exalted at the resurrection to the status of *Kyrios, Christos,* and Son of God with power (Acts 2:36; Phil. 2:9, 11; Rom. 1:4). Although there is a growing tendency in the gospel tradition to read back the messiahship into the earthly life of Jesus, the original view that the messiahship was revealed at the resurrection appearance has survived in some of the Easter pericopae. In Matt. 28:16–20 Jesus reveals himself as the exalted Son of man (cf. v. 18 with Dan. 7:14). It is possible that the Lukan pericopae also imply a revelation of Jesus as *Christos* (Luke 24:26, 46). In the Johannine Thomas pericope we have (though with a typical Johannine accentuation) a confession of the risen One as "my Lord and my God" (John 20:28). Some of the christological material now located in the earthly ministry may have belonged originally to a postresurrection setting. Bultmann, for instance, would place the baptism, confession of Peter at Caesarea Philippi, and the transfiguration in this category (see above), a view which for various reasons we are not disposed to share. On the other hand, there are grounds for supposing that the triumphant cry (Matt. 11:27; Luke 10:22) belonged originally to the postresurrection manifestation of Jesus as Son of man, as is suggested by the phrase *panta moi paredothē hypo tou patros mou* (cf. Matt. 28:18 and Dan. 7:14). At the same time, however, we must insist that although the revelation of Jesus as the exalted Messiah is postresurrectional, the messianic concept did not spring forth at Easter as a bolt from the blue. While it is true, as we have already observed, that the Gospels tend increasingly to read back an explicit messiahship into the earthly life of Jesus, a critical analysis of the earliest strata of the Gospel materials can demonstrate that Jesus at least believed himself to stand in an intimate relation with the Son of man who was to be revealed (Mark 8:38). The present writer, indeed, would go further and maintain that Jesus understood himself to be the Son of man designate. Yet the church's confession of Jesus as *Kyrios, Christos,* and so forth, is constituted not by Jesus' self-understanding, but by the Easter revelation. Easter reveals that what for Jesus was a matter of faith for the future has now been accomplished by God. By raising him from the dead God has made Jesus Lord and Christ and Son of God with power.

Next, the resurrection appearances revealed that the whole history of Jesus was the act which God had accomplished *kata tas graphas* (1 Cor. 15:3, 4). This feature is particularly emphasized in the Lukan pericope (Luke 24:32, 44), but it is also subtly present in the Fourth Gospel in what is probably traditional material (John 2:22, 12:16). The gospel tradition represents Jesus as sharing this conviction already in his earthly life (e.g., Mark 9:12; 14:21, 49 and the *dei* of the passion predictions). If such explicit teaching be historical, one is left wondering how it is to be squared with Luke 24:32, 44. Most likely it is another instance of the reading back of postresurrection faith into the earthly life of Jesus. At the same time, however, it is impossible to make sense of the whole earthly course of Jesus except on the presumption that he understood himself as called to fulfill the role of the Isaianic Servant of Yahweh. We must therefore suppose that what had been implicit in his self-understanding is made explicit by the Easter revelation. It is noteworthy that the explicit designation of Jesus as the Servant does not occur prior to the postresurrection kerygma (Acts 3:13).

It is widely held by radical critics that the redemptive interpretation of Jesus' death is postresurrectional,[11] and that all the interpretative sayings of the passion, including the *hyper* and *diathēkē logia* in the Supper narrative are *vaticinia ex eventu*. This is too large a question to examine here, but it should be observed that there is singularly little evidence that the redemptive understanding of the passion was regarded by the early church as part of the Easter revelation. Indeed, the only evidence for this is in Luke 24:26, 46. The present writer is firmly convinced that the bread- and cup-words in the Markan Supper narrative have as high a claim to authenticity as any of the undoubted logia of Jesus. What function then did the Easter revelation perform in relation to the redemptive interpretation of Christ's death? It revealed the fulfillment of what Jesus had announced as prophecy. Thus the church's faith and proclamation of the cross rests not upon the words of Jesus in themselves, but on those words as vindicated by the Easter revelation. Apart from Easter, all that the disciples could say was, "We had hoped that he was the one to redeem Israel" (Luke 24:21).

In and with this revelation of the redemptive significance of Jesus' history comes the commissioning of the *apostoloi* to proclaim it. This is a regular feature of the appearance to the Twelve in all forms, but it is also present in the traces of the appearance to Peter examined above. Similarly, the Pentecost narrative in Acts, which, as we have seen, may have been the original appearance to the five hundred, leads at once to kerygmatic witness by the whole community. The absence of this feature in Formulae II and III in 1 Corinthians 15, plus the universalistic tone of the missionary charges in the Gospel pericope have led Bultmann to suppose that the charge as such is a later accretion.[12] But although Paul does not specify the charge in 1 Corinthians 15, he nevertheless indicates in Gal. 1:10–16 that this was in fact the import of his encounter with the risen Lord. The universalistic scope of the charge is doubtless a later development, but not the charge itself. The *apostoloi* derive their sending (*apostellein*) from the risen Christ. The Lukan use of this designation for the Twelve indiscriminately before the resurrection is an anachronism. Nevertheless, there is no reason to suppose that Mark is equally guilty of anachronism when he represents the disciples as functioning as *apostoloi* occasionally during the earthly life (Mark 6:7, 30). There is an essential difference between the pre- and postresurrection sendings. Whereas the preresurrection *apostoloi* proclaim the imminence of God's eschatological act (Luke 10:9), the postresurrection *apostoloi* proclaim Jesus as Messiah, that is, they proclaim that God's eschatological act has been accomplished. Once again, however, we note that the postresurrection revelation has continuity as well as decisive discontinuity with the preresurrection life of Jesus.

As we have seen, the imparting of the Spirit was in the earliest tradition associated with the resurrection appearances, and not regarded, as in Luke 24 and Acts 1–2, as a distinct event subsequent to their termination. That the Spirit is the direct gift of the risen and exalted One is also the Pauline view. The Spirit is the Spirit of Christ and of the Lord (Rom. 1:9; 2 Cor. 3:17; Phil. 1:19; cf. Eph. 4:7ff.). The earliest church, as it were, absorbed the giving of the Spirit into the resurrection appearances, not vice versa as some contemporary scholars do when they suggest that the tradition of the appearances was the creation of the early community's experience of the Spirit. This fact is of immense theological significance. Pneumatology is dependent on Christology, not vice versa. The early Christian experience of the Spirit was not an amorphous religious enthusiasm; its form and content were derived from the work of Christ, of which the Spirit was the extender: "He will take what is mine and declare it to you" (John 16:14). Once again, we note that the postresurrection revelation of the Spirit has its roots in the history of Jesus. As C. K. Barrett has shown, the few recorded logia of Jesus about the gift of the Spirit (Mark 13:11; Luke 11:13) fail to stand the test of criticism.[13] Jesus, however, clearly understood himself to be operating under the impulsion of the Spirit, for to reject his kerygma and its authentication by signs was blasphemy against the Spirit (Mark 3:28–30; Luke 12:10). The presence of the Spirit in action in his ministry was the beginning of God's eschatological action. Believing himself to be commissioned to accomplish the decisive act through which God's eschatological action was to be accomplished, he thereby implicitly asserted that as a result of his death the Spirit would be given. His sayings about his death as the fulfillment of his baptism point in the same direction (Mark 10:38–39; Luke 12:50).

In Matt. 28:16ff. the apostolic commission includes a command to baptize (cf. also the secondary tradition in Mark 16:16). At first the evidence for this feature looks slight, late, and dubious. But it is more extensive than appears at first sight. In Luke 24:47 the missionary charge is couched in unmistakably baptismal language (*metanoian eis aphesin hamartion*), as is evident from a comparison with Acts 2:38. Again, the Johannine version of the same pericope contains the promise "If you remit (RSV: 'forgive') the sins of any, they are remitted (i.e., God has remitted them); if you retain the sins of any, they are retained." How are the remission and retention accomplished? Quite concretely by the granting or withholding of baptism on the acceptance or rejection of the kerygma. Further, the Matthean sayings about binding and loosing (Matt. 16:19 [originally a postresurrection pericope as indicated above] and Matt. 18:18 [which, as the promise in v. 20 strongly suggests, occurs in a context strongly suggestive of a postresurrection situation]) are probably baptismal in their reference. All these passages indicate that the early church understood its practice of baptism to have arisen out of the postresurrection encounters.

Again, this is not to deny that the roots of the practice lie back in the ministry of Jesus himself, and particularly, as Cullmann has argued,[14] in his interpretation of his death as a representative baptism for the many.

The earliest Christian community at Jerusalem understood itself as the *ekklesia* or *qahal* of God. It is noteworthy that the word *ekklesia* is almost completely absent from the logia of Jesus. Of the three occurrences, Matt. 18:15–19 is probably a community rule. If authentic, it could only refer to the Old Israel, though this is less likely since the contemporary Israel had ceased to understand itself as the *ekklesia*. Matthew 16:17–19 is the *tu es Petrus* passage, which, as we have seen, is best taken as a fragment of the resurrection appearance to Peter. The traditional understanding of Pentecost as the "birthday of the church" points in the same direction. *Ekklesia* means a community which understands itself as the people of God with the act of God which constitutes its being already behind it, already an accomplished fact.[15] Thus Israel of the wilderness period was an *ekklesia* (Acts 7:38), like the new Israel after the resurrection. Contemporary Israel during the lifetime of Jesus was an *'edhah,* a waiting community with the constitutive act of God still in the future. The disciples of Jesus similarly, during his earthly life, were a waiting community, waiting for the constitutive act of God in the future. They were not an *ekklesia*. The attempt to find the "thing" *ekklesia* though not the word present in the disciple band during Jesus' earthly life is misconceived.[16] All we can say is that the *promise* of the *ekklesia* was *implicit* in Jesus' assurance that his disciples would enter the kingdom as a result of his redemptive deed (Luke 12:32, 22:29). Thus, once more, it is the resurrection revelation which is constitutive of the *ekklesia;* it announces the accomplishment of what in the ministry of Jesus was still promise and prophecy.

It is curious that Cullmann, after finding the origin of Christian baptism in the historical life of Jesus, seeks the origin of the pre-Pauline Christian eucharist exclusively in the postresurrection meals of the disciples. This is a healthy reaction against the view that it stems exclusively from the last supper. Nevertheless, the last supper and the postresurrection meals need to be brought into proper relation with one another. The last supper contained a promise and prophecy of the future messianic banquet (Mark 14:25; Luke 22:17–19, cf. v. 29). The resurrection encounters reveal the actualization and fulfillment of the promise, and are thus constitutive for the reality of the eucharistic event.

Lastly, the resurrection encounters carried with them a sense of incompleteness. The eschatological reign of God had indeed been inaugurated, but it had not yet come in its fullness; it still awaited consummation. The earliest preaching of Jesus as the Messiah stood under the signature of a "not yet" and an "until" (Acts 3:21). This revelation of incompleteness is associated in the gospel tradition with the resurrection appearances (Matt. 28:20; Acts 1:6f.). This sense of incompleteness gave rise to the expectation of a return of Christ. Here again the *parousia* hope has been read back into the logia of Jesus.[17] Jesus himself had not differentiated between the exaltation of the Son of man to God and a return to earth. But from the resurrection onward, the expectation of the *parousia* remains a vital element in the kerygma. Once more, while this element of Christian faith has its roots in the historical logia of Jesus, it is constituted by the resurrection encounters. Whereas, however, according to Robinson, Jesus had envisaged an indefinite prolongation of history after his exaltation as Son of man, it would seem that it was the Easter revelation which brought home to the disciples that they must look for a *limited* prolongation of this present age until the *parousia*. It is equally possible that the earthly Jesus had envisaged an immediate consummation and that this expectation was reshaped as indicated above by the Easter revelation (cf. again Acts 1:6f.).

To sum up, therefore, while the Easter revelation in all its manifold ramifications comes not as something completely *de novo,* but as something already rooted in the mind and purpose of the Jesus of history, nevertheless that revelation is decisively constitutive for the whole of the earliest church's life and proclamation. Truly we may say with St. Paul, "If Christ has not been raised, then our preaching is in vain and your faith is in vain" (1 Cor. 15:14).

Notes

1. N. A. Dahl, *KD* 1 (1955): 104–32.

2. E. Bammel, *TZ* 11 (1955): 401–19.

3. Cf. O. Cullmann, *Christology of the New Testament* (London: SCM Press, 1954), 72ff.

4. J. Jeremias, *Die Abendmahlsworte Jesu*, 96.

5. Cf. W. Nauck, *ZNW* 47 (1956): 243–76.

6. R. Bultmann, *Geschichte der Synoptischen Tradition*, 275ff.

7. R. Bultmann, *Theology of the New Testament*, vol. 1 (London: SCM Press, 1952), 38ff.

8. Stauffer, *Theologie des Neuen Testaments*, 17, as opposed to O. Cullmann, *Peter*, 182ff.

9. Cf. most recently J. G. Davies, *He Ascended into Heaven*, 49f.

10. K. Barth, *Kirchliche Dogmatik* IV/2, 534.

11. So J. Knox, *The Death of Christ*, 77–107.

12. Bultmann, *Geschichte der Synoptischen Tradition*, 313.

13. C. K. Barrett, *The Holy Spirit in the Gospel Tradition*, 126–27, 130–32.

14. O. Cullmann, *Die Tauflehre des Neuen Testaments*, 13–17.

15. Cf. N. A. Dahl, *Das Volk Gottes, passim.*

16. Cf. the attempts of K. L. Schmidt, *TWNT* III, 523.31–526.4 and N. Flew, *Jesus and His Church*, 23–122.

17. Cf. J. Jeremias, *The Parables of Jesus*, 38–52; and J. A. T. Robinson, *Jesus and His Coming*, 83–103.

PART FOUR

The Hellenistic Jewish Mission

CHAPTER

5

THE INCARNATION IN HISTORICAL PERSPECTIVE

Who is Jesus Christ for us today? Modern Christian theologians, not least among them Albert Mollegen, have wrestled painfully with this question. Of course, there are many who think the question was settled once for all at Chalcedon, including those clerics who have rushed into print to condemn "Molle" of heresy.[1] All he had done was to insist that you cannot say "Jesus is God" except in a carefully nuanced way and with judicious qualifications. As a bald statement, it can lead one all too easily into docetism, Apollinarianism, or Eutychianism. And when one tries carefully to provide the necessary nuances and qualifications, it is quite inappropriate to level accusations of adoptionism or Nestorianism.

Systematic Christology operates with three major sets of data: the witness of the New Testament writers, the formulations of Nicea and Chalcedon, and the intellectual and cultural situation of the present day. Like all human existence, these three sets of data are historically conditioned, and to understand them we must set them in their historical situation. And, so far as the New Testament and the Christology of the councils are concerned, their findings have then to be translated into another, namely, contemporary, situation. This means among other things that just as the Nicean and Chalcedonian definitions cannot be dumped down as they are for our uncritical acceptance (though as catholic Christians, Episcopalians would certainly accept what those definitions *meant*), so, too, they cannot be used as the presuppositions for the exegesis of the New Testament. For example, we cannot understand the history of Jesus of Nazareth if we start out with the assumption that Jesus is God and man or the God-man. We may certainly want to affirm that at the end, when we have done our exegesis, as a confession of faith. But that is another matter.

The Prayer of Jesus

Accordingly, we will examine the Christologies of the evangelists from a quite limited perspective. We will start with Jesus of Nazareth as a first-century Jew who prayed. That he did so is the claim of all the evangelists and of nearly every stratum of the gospel tradition.[2] It is therefore a historical datum that passes the criterion of multiple attestation.

The gospel traditions and the redaction of the evangelists develop this historical fact of Jesus' prayer in different directions. Mark has Jesus pray in moments of crisis. He prays after the day of successful healings in Capernaum. For the Marcan Jesus this represents a crisis; the continuation of the Capernaum ministry would expose him to the temptation of presenting himself in terms of a *theios anēr*. Simon, as the mouthpiece of that Christology,[3] tries to call Jesus back but, strengthened by his prayer, Jesus rejects the temptation. Again, Jesus prays after the feeding of the five thousand, a critical moment which again exposed him to a similar temptation. Finally, he prays at Gethsemane, and embraces the cross against all other alternative Christologies.

In the first instance, Luke appears to extend the crisis prayers. Jesus prays at his baptism,[4] before the call of the Twelve,[5] and during the transfiguration.[6] Luke elaborates the Gethsemane prayer, perhaps drawing upon his special tradition.[7] The third evangelist, however, has carefully dismantled the polemical thrust in Jesus' prayer as portrayed by Mark.[8] Unlike Mark, Luke has no qualms about presenting Jesus as a *theios anēr*. His whole ministry is carried out in the power of the Spirit and—closely connected with the idea of *pneuma*—by the *dynamis* of God. This *dynamis* is drained from

him through his miraculous activity.[9] Such notions account for
Luke's redactional addition of a reference to Jesus' prayer after the
healing of the leper,[10] and again after the feeding of the multitude.
Mark had used Jesus' quest for privacy as part of his messianic
secrecy motif. For Luke, the quest for privacy is a means of refresh-
ment and strengthening for ministry. It is through his prayer that
the Lucan Jesus operates as the channel of God's presence and
action.

The Fourth Gospel has the most developed theology of Jesus'
prayer. The major example is in the high priestly prayer of John 17,
a more elaborate form of the type of prayer featured in the special
Lucan material. But the most important reference to Jesus' prayer is
in John 11:41b–42. The passage reads as follows:

> Jesus lifted up his eyes and said: "Father, I thank thee that
> thou hast heard me. I know thou hearest me always, but I
> have said this on account of the people standing by, that they
> may believe that thou didst send me."

At first sight, this seems to say that Jesus had no need to pray at all,
but did so only to impress the bystanders, a not very attractive picture, indeed a rather offensive one. Bultmann, however, has given
a most helpful interpretation of this passage which deserves far
more notice than it has received:

> Jesus' prayer therefore is the demonstration of that which he
> has constantly said about himself, that he is nothing of him-
> self. But does it not, thereby, become a spectacle, a farce? It
> is obvious that Jesus' words in vv. 41f. are not heard by the
> bystanders; they only see his attitude of prayer, and in this
> situation they must understand his prayer as one of request.
> Are they deceived? No, for it is the request of one who
> stands in perfect unity with the Father. That he stands be-
> fore God as a petitioner is shown by the fact that the Father's
> attitude to him is described as *akouein* (*ēkousas mou*); if he
> knows that the Father constantly hears (*pantote mou akoueis*),
> it is implied that he, the Son, *never steps out of the attitude of
> the petitioner, but continually holds fast to it.* For this reason

he does not need to be quickened out of a prayerless attitude
to make petition by means of a particular act; rather when,
in a particular situation, he recalls to consciousness his relation to God as that of one who makes requests, his request
must immediately change to thanks. For he who knows
himself to be perpetually in the attitude of a petitioner before God cannot do other than recognize himself as a man to
whom God perpetually gives gifts. But correspondingly, he
cannot know himself as one perpetually heard if he does not
know himself as one perpetually asking. The character of
this communion with God is clearly delineated by this: *He
does not need to make petitions like others, who have to rouse
themselves out of their attitude of prayerlessness and therefore god-
lessness; for he continually stands before God as the petitioner and
therefore as the receiver.* [11]

On this interpretation Jesus' vocal prayer is the surfacing of
an inner, hidden activity which is going on all the time. It is the
continuous traffic between the Father and the Son, between
heaven and earth, which Nathanael will see as he witnesses the
earthly life of Jesus. For he will see the heavens opened in Jesus'
prayer (as they were first opened at the baptism!) and the angels of
God ascending and descending upon the Son of man (John 1:51). It
is the ground base, the *cantus firmus,* of all his words and deeds. It is
in this inner, hidden activity that the relation of the Father and the
Son is continually actualized. Hence Jesus' overt prayer is a public
manifestation of that ongoing relationship. That is why it demon-
strates to the bystanders that the Father sent the Son. For the sending of the Son, while inaugurated in Jesus' initial call, has to be
constantly renewed in his prayer.

The Fourth Gospel contains many references to the relationship between the Father and the Son. In the light of John 11:41b–42
these should be interpreted on the background of the Johannine understanding of Jesus' prayer.

First, John the Baptist bears testimony to the inner significance of Jesus' baptism: "I saw the Spirit descend as a dove from
heaven and it remained upon him" (John 1:32). The evangelist sees
no conflict between the initial assertion that the Word became

flesh and the later statement that the Spirit descended on Jesus only at his baptism. This suggests that the two events are identical. In the Spirit's descent upon Jesus the Word begins to be enfleshed. But again, this enfleshment is not a once-for-all event. The Spirit inaugurates the Father-Son relationship through which the Son is called to speak the words and do the works of the Father. The Son responds in obediences to this call and is empowered to fulfill this mission. The Spirit "abides" upon Jesus. That is to say, the relationship of the Father and the Son is continually actualized again and again in the career of the Son. After this inaugural event, not related but attested by the Baptist, Jesus is introduced on the stage of history by a succession of titles. He is the elect of God (1:34); the Lamb of God (1:36 cf. 29); Rabbi (1:38); Messiah (1:41); Son of God (1:49); King of Israel (1:49); Son of man (1:51). All of these titles may be regarded as expositions of the hearing of the baptismal call, for they expound the witness of the Baptist (1:19–34) and the acceptance of that witness by some of the Baptist's followers (1:35–51).

History and Mythology in the Fourth Gospel

The ensuing dialogues and discourses include among other themes an exposition of the Father-Son Christology, and therefore of the relationship which according to chapter 1 was inaugurated in Jesus' initial endowment with the Spirit and which, as we have seen from John 11:41b–42, is constantly renewed in his prayer.

The Father "sent" the Son.[12] Much of the "sending" language is clearly susceptible, even in the Fourth Gospel,[13] to a historical interpretation, as it is in the synoptic tradition (e.g., Matt. 15:24; Luke 4:43). For John the Baptist was also sent from God (John 1:6; cf. 2:38), and after his glorification the Son sends his disciples as the Father had sent him. "From God," "from above" (3:31), and "from heaven" (3:31c) need not by themselves mean more than the source of the Son's historical authorization. This authorization is alluded to in contexts which make it quite clear that its source lies in the historical event of the baptism.

Whether John 3:31–36 is still part of the Baptist's speech or is an appended Johannine meditation, it serves as comment on Jesus' baptism. This discourse identifies the Son's sending with his endowment with the Spirit (3:34) in language derived from the heavenly voice of the baptism. References to the authorization of Jesus are also expressed in language derived from the tradition of the Son of man's enthronement at his exaltation: the Father gave all things into his hands (3:35; cf. 5:22). It is this historical authorization, responded to in obedience, that enables the Son to speak the words (i.e., the Johannine discourses) and to do the works (i.e., the Johannine signs) of the Father. Even the language which speaks of the Father's sending the Son "into the world" (3:17) is open to a historical interpretation, since the disciples themselves are likewise sent into the world after the accomplishment of Jesus' historical mission (John 17:18). The historical nature of the sending and its baptismal connection comes out clearly even in John 6. For the Father's "sealing" of the Son (v. 27) is unquestionably baptismal. This is particularly surprising and significant in the chapter which, as we will see, introduces for the first time an unmistakably mythological Christology.

Like the language of sending, that of the Son's "coming" is patient of a historical interpretation.[14] For the Baptist also "comes" (1:7; 1:31), just as "another" may come in his own name (5:43), as thieves and robbers have come before the Son (John 10:8, 10) and as wolves will come after him (10:12). Even when it says the Son came "from above" and "from heaven," this is capable of referring in the first instance to his historical authorization (3:31).

The language which speaks of the Father's "giving" the Son (John 3:16) is likewise historical. Its roots lie in the early kerygmatic (*para*)*didonai* formula which spoke of the Son's being delivered up (reverential passive) in the passion (Mark 9:31, etc.; Rom. 4:25). In the Fourth Gospel this (*para*)*didonai* is extended to cover Jesus' history in its totality.

Side by side with this historical language there begins to appear at John 3:13 another type of language which is distinctly mythological. We hear there of the "descent" of the Son of man from heaven. But it is in the bread discourse of John 6 that this mythological thought is developed.

First, the Johannine Jesus speaks of the bread that came (comes) down from heaven (6:32–33). Next, he identifies himself with this bread in the first of the seven "I am" sayings (6:41, 45). Finally, he drops the identification formula and speaks ostensibly of himself as a mythological being who came down from heaven (6:38, cf. v. 41). This usage is echoed later in the high priestly prayer (17:5). As a result, all the previous historical language becomes ambiguous. Is the apparently historical language to be interpreted mythologically?[15] How are the historical and the mythological to be reconciled?

Traditional orthodoxy has unconsciously solved this problem by transposing Johannine mythology into the metaphysical conceptuality of Nicea and Chalcedon and then interpreting the historical language in metaphysical terms. But this fails to do justice to the historical quality of that language and creates an insoluble problem of which it was blithely unaware. For why should the eternal Son need to be endowed with the Spirit at his baptism if he already existed in two natures? Why should he receive a historical authorization, and why should he pray to the Father if that prayer was not ordinary human petition but a prayer which was constitutive of his christological role?

When Bultmann recognized the mythological character of the ascent-descent language and discovered its source in his pre-Christian gnostic redeemer myth, he correctly perceived the problem created by the juxtaposition of the two languages, historical and mythological. The solution he offered was to invoke the pre-Pauline and Pauline Christology of kenosis.[16] This answer, however, was unacceptable because the Fourth Gospel presents the incarnation not as a kenosis or *krypsis* (concealment) of the divine glory but precisely as its manifestation.[17] Käsemann rightly saw this but unwittingly fell back on the procedure of traditional orthodoxy and allowed the historical language once more to be swallowed up by the mythological. Thus he accused the Fourth Gospel of a "naive docetism."[18] The Johannine Christ strode about the earth like a god. He was a heavenly being who briefly touched down on earth, assuming a human guise merely to reveal his glory, and went back to heaven. Luise Schottroff went further and accused the fourth evangelist of an out-and-out gnostic-docetist Christology.[19] Once again these solutions fail to give due weight to the historical language.

How then will we solve the dilemma? It is significant that the mythological language begins with the identification of Jesus with the bread from heaven, the heavenly manna. As Raymond E. Brown has shown,[20] this typology is rooted in the wisdom tradition. By identifying himself with the bread from heaven, the Johannine Jesus presents himself as the spokesman and embodiment of the divine wisdom. This is the clue to the descent-ascent saying in which the Johannine Jesus speaks in the first person (John 6:38). The ego here is the ego of the divine wisdom. It is also the clue to such sayings as "before Abraham was, I am" (8:58). One can understand this startling claim if it is a saying of the heavenly wisdom, a pronouncement of the kind one would expect to find on the lips of wisdom in the sapiential literature of the Old Testament and Apocrypha.[21] This interpretation is exactly the same as that proposed by M. J. Suggs[22] for the Matthean invitation, "Come to me, all who labor and are heavy laden, and I will give you rest. Take my yoke upon you, and learn from me: for I am gentle and lowly of heart, and you will find rest for your souls. For my yoke is easy and my burden is light" (Matt. 11:28–30). Jesus' historical humanity is not absorbed by the wisdom mythology. It remains unimpaired. As a man he is called by God to the historical mission of incarnating the wisdom/logos in his word and work. He responds to that call by his continuing prayer. His words and deeds are thus the words and deeds of the Father. When he speaks, he speaks as the Father's wisdom which speaks through him, and when he acts, his deeds are the works of the heavenly wisdom.

This gives a typically Johannine two-level character to all the self-predicates of Jesus. In some sayings, the historical sending and coming sayings, the primary ego is that of the historical Jesus. But they acquire a second level in reference to the coming of the wisdom/logos into the world from heaven in and through the sending and coming of the historical Jesus. This explains, for instance, the symbolic interpretation of the footwashing as a parable of the Son's coming from God and returning to him (John 13:3), a saying which speaks *both* of the mission and crucifixion of Jesus *and* of the entry of wisdom into the world and her subsequent return to heaven. This two-level meaning further explains such sayings as "I and the Father are one" (John 10:30) and "he who has seen me has seen the Father" (14:9). It further explains the six great "I am" sayings which follow upon the initial self-identification of Jesus with the bread from heaven (8:12; 10:7; 10:11; 11:25; 14:6; 15:1). The "I am" sayings are properly self-predicates of wisdom, whose spokesman and embodiment, however, is Jesus. They involve a kind of *communicatio idiomatum*. What is predicable of wisdom is predicable of Jesus and vice versa.

It is significant that the bread discourse forms the crucial turning point in John's christological interpretation. It is here that the mythological background of Jesus' historical mission comes first to the fore, and the two-level character of all of Jesus' self-predications is exposed. It is here that the first "I am" saying occurs.

Friedrich Gogarten[23] correctly perceived the two-level character of Johannine Christology. He observed that there are two events, an event between God and Jesus in history, and an event between the Father and the Son in eternity. These events are one and the same. We would slightly amend Gogarten's formulation, for the Father-Son relationship appears on the historical side. We prefer to say that the historical event of call and response between the Father and the Son reflects the eternal relationship between God and his heavenly wisdom. The point of intersection between the two levels is Jesus' baptism and his ongoing prayer.

John's Gospel and the Patristic Christology

John's two-level Christology is the equivalent in historical terms of the metaphysical doctrine of the two natures. The Nicean doctrine of the deity of the preexistent Son is a translation into metaphysical terms of the Fourth Gospel's mythological proclamation of Jesus as the incarnation of the preexistent divine wisdom. We are entitled to recognize these later credal affirmations as legitimate attempts to translate the historical and mythological languages of the New Testament into the metaphysical language of the fourth and fifth centuries. What cannot be permitted is the insistence that the metaphysical language must be used as a presupposition for the exegesis of the New Testament. John's Gospel must not be interpreted in the light of the later metaphysics; the later metaphysics must be interpreted in the light of John's Gospel.

There are two remaining difficulties. The Nicene Creed locates the incarnation at the nativity: "And was incarnate by the Holy Ghost of the Virgin Mary." John's Gospel, as we have seen, regards the incarnation as a historical process inaugurated at Jesus' baptism. "The Word became flesh" is a comment on the whole history which the evangelist is about to relate, beginning with the baptism and running through the signs and discourses which are to follow, and culminating in Jesus' glorification through his passion.[24] How does one relate John to Nicea? The second difficulty is, How does one avoid an adoptionist interpretation of Johannine Christology? The second question can be answered without serious difficulty. The Johannine Christology is emphatic that the whole history of Jesus rested on the divine initiative. God called Jesus for his mission at the moment of his baptism. This call was constantly renewed in Jesus' prayer. The second question is more serious, and the answer will depend on an investigation of the infancy narratives and on a relation of their Christology to that of the Fourth Gospel.

Notes

1. See Dr. Mollegen's letter to the editor in *The Living Church* (May 11, 1975) and the subsequent correspondence.

2. References to Jesus' prayer occur in the pre-Marcan tradition (Gethsemane, a christological story compiled from various materials including the Lord's Prayer), Q (the Lord's Prayer—what Jesus taught his disciples he must first have prayed himself), Special Luke (Jesus'

intercession for his disciples, Luke 22:32), the pre-Johannine tradition (the "Johannine Gethsemane," John 12:27–28, also modeled on the Lord's Prayer). For the connection between Jesus' baptismal call and his use of Abba, see J. Jeremias, *New Testament Theology,* I (New York: Charles Scribner's Sons, 1971), 51–56, 67–68.

3. See T. Weeden, *Mark: Traditions in Conflict* (Philadelphia: Fortress Press, 1971), passim. One need not accept Weeden's thesis in the extreme form in which he stated it. Although mouthpieces of a *theios anēr* Christology during the earthly ministry, the disciples are converted to Marcan orthodoxy at the resurrection (Mark 9:9; 14:28; 16:7).

4. Luke 3:21. If Q contained a baptismal narrative (so Streeter, Taylor, and more recently J. M. Robinson, "Basic Shifts in German Theology," *Interpretation* 16 [1962]: 76–97, esp. 82f.), it would be consistent with the *Gattung* of Q if it began with sayings of Jesus about his baptism, which appoints him the spokesman of the divine wisdom. See J. M. Robinson and H. Koester, *Trajectories Through Early Christianity* (Philadelphia: Fortress Press, 1971), 71–113.

5. Luke 6:12, either Lucan redaction or from Special Luke (T. Schramm, *Der Markus-Stoff bei Lukas* [Cambridge: Cambridge University Press, 1971], 113).

6. Luke 9:28. Again this may be Special Luke rather than Lucan redaction. So Schramm, *Markus-Stoff,* 136–39.

7. So Streeter, Taylor. One does not need to accept their proto-Luke theory. Luke in any case had special passion traditions which he supplemented from Mark.

8. Especially see Luke's redaction of Jesus' flight, Mark 1:35–38 = Luke 4:42–43. In Luke it is not Simon, the Marcan mouthpiece of *theios anēr* Christology, but the crowd that pursues Jesus. In Luke the flight is motivated not by a rejection of false Christology but by the desire to extend the activities of the *theios anēr* further afield. Luke accordingly shifts Mark 1:35 to 5:16 where it better serves that Christology.

9. This idea was already present in Mark's miracle source (Mark 5:30), but Mark toned it down by shifting the emphasis to the woman's faith.

10. See above, n. 8.

11. R. Bultmann, *The Gospel of John* (Philadelphia: Westminster Press, 1971), 408. Translation modified.

12. *Apostellō* in reference to Jesus is unequivocally historical prior to 6:38 in: John 3:34 (see below); 5:36, 38; 6:29. *Pempō* occurs prior to John 6:38 in reference to Jesus' historical sending at: 4:34, where "doing the will" refers to Jesus' historical activity; 5:23, 24; 5:36 (in the

context of the Father's witness, which began with the voice at the baptism, continued in Jesus' prayer, and surfaced at the "Johannine Gethsemane," John 12:28).

13. Especially if the prologue was added subsequently to the composition of the Gospel. See B. Lindars, *The Gospel of John*, Century Bible, rev. (London: Oliphants, 1972), 76f.

14. *Erchomai* is clearly historical at 1:15, 27 (the Baptist's witness). 3:2 refers to the source of Jesus' authorization, not to a mythological origin. Cf. 4:25.

15. After John 6:38, *apostellō* occurs in an ambiguous sense at 7:29; 8:42; 10:36; 11:42; 17:3. Sometimes the primary reference is still historical (e.g., 10:36 occurs in a context which alludes to Jesus' baptismal consecration). *Pempō* is ambiguous at 6:38, 39, 44, where the context suggests a primary reference to Jesus' descent from heaven, and at 7:18, where the primary reference is historical (Jesus' baptismal authorization). 8:16, 8:29 occur in a context which alludes to the Father's witness, and are therefore primarily historical, as also is 9:4. In 12:44 the allusion is primarily mythological as v. 46 shows, but in 12:49 historical (Jesus' obedience to the Father's commandment). *Erchomai* is primarily historical at 7:27, 28 (7:41); 10:10b. It is ambiguous at 8:14, 8:42, and 18:37, though the preceding reference to Jesus' birth suggests here historical mission. The references to Jesus' "coming into the world" at 9:39 and 11:27 are primarily historical; those at 12:46 and 16:28 are primarily mythological. *Exerchomai* is ambiguous at 8:42, but with a primary reference to Jesus' authorization. At 13:3; 16:28; 16:30; and 17:8 it is primarily mythological.

16. Bultmann, *Gospel of John*, at 1:14. Cf. idem, *Theology of the New Testament*, vol. 2 (New York: Charles Scribner's Sons, 1955), 40–49. Bultmann loves to speak of the "paradox" of the Word becoming flesh.

17. The *doxa* of God is manifested (*phaneroō*) in Jesus' ministry: John 2:11; cf. 1:14; 11:4 (12:41?); 17:22 (17:24?).

18. E. Käsemann, *The Testament of Jesus* (Philadelphia: Fortress Press, 1968), 8–13.

19. L. Schottroff, *Der Glaubende und die feindliche Welt* (Neukirchen: Neukirchner Verlag, 1970). This one-sided interpretation can appeal to the fact that during the second century prior to Irenaeus it was the gnostics who appreciated the Fourth Gospel; see W. von Loewenich, *Das Johannesverständnis im zweiten Jahrhundert*, BZNW 13 (1932); W. Bauer, *Orthodoxy and Heresy in Earliest Christianity* (Philadelphia: Fortress Press, 1971); E. M. Pagels, *The Johannine Gospel in Gnostic Exegesis* (Nashville: Abingdon Press, 1973).

20. See R. E. Brown, *The Gospel of John*, Anchor Bible 29 (Garden City, NY: Doubleday & Co., 1966), 272–75.

21. In this literature, wisdom activated Israel's salvation history including Abraham (Sir. 44:19–21). There are frequent self-predicates of wisdom in this literature, beginning with Prov. 8:24. See Bultmann, *Gospel of John*, 327 n. 5. Bultmann rightly sees that Jesus is speaking not in his own capacity but as a spokesman of the gnostic revelation. His assumption, however, of a pre-Christian gnostic redeemer myth has been shattered by the researches of Colpe and others. See Robinson, "Basic Shifts," and W. Meeks, *The Prophet-King*, SNT 14 (Leiden: E. J. Brill, 1967), 12–17. For the gnostic redeemer myth we now substitute the Palestinian-Hellenistic-Jewish wisdom myth.

22. See M. J. Suggs, *Wisdom, Law and Christology in Matthew's Gospel* (Cambridge: Harvard University Press, 1971), 71–97.

23. F. Gogarten, *Demythologizing and History* (London: SCM Press, 1955), 72. The German title, *Entmythologisierung und Kirche,* carried a primary allusion to Bultmann's controversy with the Lutheran orthodoxy of the fifties, but suggested also a contrast between historical thinking and the metaphysics of patristic orthodoxy.

24. C. K. Barrett in conversation (May 1975) expressed the opinion that the aorist *egeneto* (John 1:14) must be punctiliar. But in Hellenistic Greek, that aorist can also be *"complexive,"* i.e., expressing "linear actions which (having been completed) are regarded as a whole" (F. Blass & A. Debrunner, *A Greek Grammar of the New Testament and Other Early Christian Literature*. Tr. Robert W. Funk (Chicago: University of Chicago Press, 1961), 33.

6

NEW TESTAMENT ROOTS
TO THE THEOTOKOS

Introduction

My assigned title advisedly uses the word "roots"—and perhaps
with an even wider appropriateness, for 1978 is the year of concern
with roots. Alex Haley would not claim or want to claim that he
himself was an exact reproduction of Kunta Kinte. But he would
claim that there is some continuity between him and his African
ancestor. We should look then, not to "prove" the legitimacy of
theotokos from scripture, but rather to see whether there is any continuity between the christological affirmations of the NT, especially in connection with Jesus' birth, and the later christological
doctrine of the *theotokos*.

Apart from its mariological implications, which are theologically and historically secondary, the *theotokos* poses two major
questions. One concerns the *origin* of Jesus (represented by the
tokos), and the other concerns his divinity or deity (represented
by the *theo-*). In order to explore the New Testament roots of
this term, we will investigate first what the New Testament has
to say about the origin of Jesus and then what it has to say about
his deity.

The Origin of Jesus

The very early christological formulae[1] had very little to say about Jesus' origin. They were concerned with what Jesus had "become" (the word is placed in quotation marks because the question is raised in functional rather than in ontological terms).[2] Jesus is described in the Pentecost speech of Peter as "a man attested by God, whom the Jews crucified but whom God has made Lord and Christ." This formula is often called adoptionist, as though Jesus was a man who was made divine at the resurrection. However, not only do the postresurrection titles indicate that it is a new function rather than a new nature (as we have already noted above) that is given to the exalted One, but already his earthly life was initiated and made operative by God. Jesus was "a man *attested by God* with mighty works and wonders which God did through him in your midst" (Acts 2:22). A similar formula in a later kerygmatic speech makes the same point: "he went about doing good and healing all that were oppressed by the devil, for *God was with him*" (Acts 10:38). These early "adoptionist" formulae do not even suggest that an ordinary man was elevated to messianic function. Already in his earthly appearance Jesus had a special relation to God: God "attested" him, or God "was with him." The same is true of another early pre-Pauline[3] "adoptionist" formula which underlies Rom. 1:3. It reads:

> (Jesus) who was descended from David according to the flesh, and appointed Son of God in power. . . .

Here we have a contrast between Son of David (a designation of Jesus in his earthly existence) and the new function as Son of God to which he was appointed at his resurrection. He was already "Son of David" in his earthly life. Moreover, this formula alludes for the first time to his birth (*genomenon* = having come into being as the Son of David) as a christological "moment."

The next pattern[4] is one which expresses God's "sending" Jesus into history. It is to be found at Gal. 4:4 in what is probably a pre-Pauline formula, which reads:

> God sent forth his Son
> born of a woman
>
> . . . .
>
> that we might receive the adoption of sons.

There exists today a strong consensus[5] that the origin of this sending pattern is to be sought in the wisdom mythology as developed particularly in Hellenistic Judaism.[6] This means that the "Son" in this pattern is understood as a preexistent figure.[7] Until recently I shared this view myself.[8] However, I have been led to reconsider this thesis for a number of reasons. First, where the wisdom background is operative, it is usually to say something about either the mode of existence of the preexistent One (Phil. 2:6) or his preexistent activity (Col. 1:15–17; Heb. 1:2b–3a) or both (John 1:1–3). Second, it has been questioned in another connection whether the idea of "sending" in connection with wisdom is really an aspect of Jewish sophiology. In the normal form of the myth, wisdom "comes" on her own initiative.[9] Third, I find a closer analogy between Gal. 4:4 and the sending of the son in the parable of the vineyard (Mark 12:1–9 para.) than with the sophiological hymns. In both cases we are speaking of a historical appearance which is initiated with God. The nearest analogy for this is God's "sending" of the prophets. Thus I would now argue that the sending pattern will have a salvation-historical rather than a sophiological background. As God raised up and sent prophets in the course of Israel's salvation history, so finally God sends his Son. Of course this is a unique sending, to be distinguished from the sending of the prophets, for this is God's unique and final act of sending. But I don't think that in the sending pattern christological reflection has got beyond the uniqueness of this emissary in salvation history. Remember, we are talking here of the pre-Pauline sending pattern: it is highly probable that Paul himself, who also, as we will see, drew upon the sophiological hymns, reinterpreted the sending pattern in the light of the preexistent concept which those hymns involve. A similar sending pattern Christology is echoed in Rom. 8:3, which reads:

> sending his son in the likeness of sinful flesh.

This too is probably a pre-Pauline schema,[10] similar to the one in Gal. 4:4. Once again, Paul himself probably interpreted it in terms of his preexistence Christology; indeed, the emphasis upon the Son's assumption of the "likeness of sinful flesh" suggests a little more strongly the presumption that he had previously existed in a state without the flesh.

One more point is to be noticed. Let us return to Rom. 1:3. Paul prefaces this formula with the phrase "his Son." This brings that formula into conformity with the sending schema: it is now God's Son who is being sent into the world, although Paul retains the thought that he embarked upon a new stage of his sonship at the resurrection.

It is interesting and significant to see how Paul can combine two different christological traditions of varying origin, the Son of David Christology and the sending-of-the Son Christology. This is an important fact with wide implications. It supports our contention that Paul himself could have combined the Son-sending schema with his other christological pattern of preexistence. It explains how the infancy narratives, to which we are coming in a moment, could combine the Son of David Christology and the sending-of-the-Son Christology. And most important of all, it will facilitate our understanding of the combination of the virginal conception with the preexistence Christology in the post–New Testament period.

Recall for a moment that Son in the pre-Pauline sending pattern will still refer, not to metaphysical quality, but to the role which is to be played in salvation history. It is in this connection that the coming into being or birth of the Son becomes a christological moment (*genomenou*, Rom. 1:3; *genomenon* Gal. 4:4). What by implication in this passage the mother of Jesus bore was One who was destined to play a unique role in salvation history. There is no reflection upon preexistence or upon the state in which he preexisted. And though it is a christological moment, the birth is essentially preparatory for his future role.

A more clearly defined account of the origin of Jesus is given in the infancy narratives of Matthew and Luke, particularly in the annunciation stories in those Gospels.[11] Here conception/birth is considerably enhanced as a christologically significant moment. We are not here concerned with the virginal conception, but with *what* it was that Mary conceived and bore, or rather with what the christological significance was of what Mary conceived and bore.

The birth narrative in Matthew brings together a number of christological titles accorded to the child whom Mary bore. It is not certain whether "Christos" in Matt. 1:18 is intended as a christological title, or whether by this time it has become practically a proper name. The angel's address to Joseph, "son of David," and Joseph's acceptance of the child of Mary into his family indicate that Mary's child is also a son of David. The name "Jesus" has a soteriological import: he will save his people from their sins. This name "Jesus" is further explicated in the citation formula, added as a comment by the evangelist, to mean "Emmanuel," which he further translated for the readers' benefit as "God with us" (Matt. 1:23). After the birth of the child, the magi come seeking him who was "born *king* of the Jews" (Matt. 2:2), and the evangelist goes on to indicate that king here means the Christ, the Messiah (Matt. 2:4). The formula citation added by the evangelist to the narrative of the flight into Egypt, "out of Egypt have I called my son," indicates further that the child is the Son of God. The whole system of formula quotations employed by Matthew indicates that the birth of Mary's child is interpreted to mean the entrance into the world of the salvific event to which the whole of Israel's salvation history had pointed.

Mary therefore gives birth to the Messiah, the King of the Jews, the one who will be the Savior of his people, the Son of God, and Emmanuel, meaning "God with us." It is clear particularly from the tense of the verb in the quotation "he *will save* his people from their sins," that all of these titles have reference not to the ontological quality of the child in a preexistent state or even at the moment of conception or birth, but to the role he will play in salvation history. This is true even of the title "Emmanuel." It would be an anachronism to interpret Matthew's meaning to be that Jesus is ontologically identical with God.[12] He is the one through whom God's presence will become available to his people through his salvific work. The final fulfillment of this promise comes when the exalted One declares to his disciples at the end of the Gospel, "Lo, I am with you always, to the close of the ages" (Matt. 28:20). That in the Matthean birth narrative we are still within the orbit of salvation history and of functional Christology is further indicated by the annunciation genre in which the birth of Mary's child is first proclaimed. For the annunciation pattern is a regular Old Testament device to convey the role the child to be born will play in salvation history.

The case is very similar with the Lucan birth narrative. The Lucan annunciation story even more clearly than Matthew's expresses that what is being announced is the future role of the child in salvation history:

> He will be great, and will be called the son of the
>   Most High,
> and the Lord God will give him the throne of his
>   father David,
> and he will reign over the house of Jacob for ever;
> and of his kingdom there will be no end.
> *(Luke 1:32–33)*

The future, functional salvation-historical character of the title "Son" is to be read equally into the second promise of the angel:

> therefore the child to be born will be called holy,
> the Son of God.
> *(Luke 1:35)*

He is to be called these things because of the salvation he is to accomplish in history, not because of his inherent nature.

In the visitation story Mary is greeted by Elizabeth as "the mother of my Lord" (Luke 1:43). It is very striking that a messianic title of majesty is attributed to the unborn child by another human being. Given the idea of the messianic secret, there is of course no question that this is a historical record. In fact, the verse is probably redactional.[13] Luke permits the same title of majesty to be ascribed to the child in the angelic announcement of his birth:

For to you is born this day in the city of David a Savior who
is Christ the Lord.

The conjunction of *kyrios* with the other titles *Christos* and *Sōtēr*
indicates that we are still within the realm of functional and historical Christology which speaks of the unique and final role the child
is to play in salvation history. Since Luke is at pains throughout his
birth narratives to demonstrate the superiority of the role of Jesus
over John the Baptist in salvation history, Elizabeth's salutation can
clearly mean Luke's intention, no more than just that.

We need not concern ourselves with the virginal conception as
such.[14] But we need to note that it is a narrative way of affirming
the Christology of the sending pattern. The emphasis lies on the
pneumatic origin of the conception. The whole history of Jesus has
its origin in an act of God: it is "*Gottgewirkt.*" The conceptual birth
is a christological moment, but only as a prelude for the Christ event
as a whole. The other major aspect of the infancy narratives, the
Davidic sonship, which has often been thought to be contradictory
to the virginal conception, had already been combined with the
sending-of-the-Son pattern in Rom. 1:3–4, so it should not pose
any particular problem here.

The preexistence-incarnation Christology is a third way of
expressing Jesus' transcendental origin. Perhaps the earliest literary
appearance of this Christology is in 1 Cor. 8:6, where Paul speaks
of "the Lord Jesus Christ, through whom are all things and through
whom we exist." This implies that there was incarnated in Jesus
Christ a preexistent reality which had acted as the agent of creation. There is as we have seen already a growing consensus that
the source of this concept is to be sought in the development of the
idea of wisdom in Hellenistic Judaism.[15] Paul also identifies Christ
with the wisdom of God already in 1 Cor. 1:30, and in his exegesis
of the rock in the exodus story in 1 Cor. 10:4 Paul may also be
identifying Christ as the incarnation of wisdom who has previously
been active in Israel's salvation history.[16]

But the clearest expression of the preexistence-incarnation
pattern in the homologoumena is to be found in Phil. 2:6–11,
which is usually (and in my opinion correctly) designated a

pre-Pauline hymn with slight Pauline modifications.[17] For our purposes the important part of the hymn reads:

> (who) being in the form of God
> did not count equality with God
> a thing to be clung to[18]
>
> but emptied himself,
> having taken the form of a servant
> having become (*genomenos*) in the likeness of human being.
>
> *Phil. 2:6–7*

This hymn expresses a Christology quite different from the sending-of-the-Son pattern. It speaks in mythological rather than salvation-historical terms of the preexistence of a heavenly being in a mode of existence equal to that of God himself. It speaks further of the entrance of the preexistent One into history as an act undertaken by his own initiative, rather than as an act initiated by God. But like the sending-of-the-Son pattern, it identifies the birth of the incarnate One as a christological moment (cf. the *genomenon* of Phil. 2:7 with the *genomenon* of Gal. 4:4). This shows that although the two Christologies are quite distinct in origin, a potentiality exists for their combination, just as the Son of David and sending-of-the-Son Christologies had already been combined in Rom. 1:3–4. There is a further point to be made. Like the sending-of-the-Son Christology, the stress lies upon the soteriological goal: the divine mode of existence is mentioned only because the preexistent One surrendered it, emptied himself, and humbled himself in a life culminating in death, a death which has the soteriological effect of subjugating the cosmic powers of evil. This shows that although this Christology introduces an ontic and a cosmological-speculative element into consideration, its purpose is similar to that of the earlier Christologies, namely, to affirm the soteriological significance of the Christ event in its totality.

The next wisdom hymn to be examined occurs in the possibly deutero-Pauline Col. 1:15–17f. It reads:

> He is the image of the invisible God
> the firstborn of all creation;
> for in him all things were created.
>
> . . . .
>
> He is before all things,
> and in him all things hold together.

This hymn, like the Philippians hymn, affirms the preexistence of the Redeemer ("firstborn of all creation"; "he is before all things"). Like the Philippians hymn, it too speaks, though in somewhat different language (*eikōn* instead of *morphē*), of the divine mode of being of the preexistent One. But unlike the Philippians hymn, it stresses the activity of the preexistent One as the agent of creation ("through him all things were created . . . all things were created through him") and of preservation ("in him all things hold together"). This idea was already present in the Pauline homologoumena (1 Cor. 8:6). But the most important difference is that this hymn does not speak of the entry into the world of the preexistent One. Yet it is implied, for the next stanza goes on to say that he is resurrected from the dead and becomes the head of the church.

The third preexistence hymn is in Heb. 1:2. It reads:

> (a Son) whom he appointed heir of all things,
> through whom also he created the world.
> He reflects the glory of God
> and bears the very stamp of his nature.

Again we notice similarities and differences with the other hymns. The preexistent One's divine mode of being is again affirmed, again in slightly different language (*apaugasma tēs doxēs* and *charaktēr*) but still derived from the wisdom mythology. It states that the preexistent One was the agent of creation ("through whom he created the world). Like the Colossians hymn it goes on to imply, but does not explicitly assert, the entry of the preexistent One into history ("when he had made purification for sins"). But the most important point to note about this hymn is that it identifies the preexistent One with the Son of God and speaks of the Son as the culmination of God's revelatory activity in the prophets. Here we may see a real combination of the sending-of-the-Son Christology with the wisdom Christology (note that nothing is said here of the Son's initiative, an indication that the author of Hebrews ascribes the initiative to God).

The final hymn to be considered is the prologue to John's Gospel. The relevant portions are:

> In the beginning was the Word,
> and the Word was with God,
> and the Word was God.
>
> He was in the beginning with God;
>
> all things were made through him,
> and without him was not anything made that was
>   made . . .
> and the Word became flesh,
> and dwelt among us.

Once again we see the familiar wisdom themes: the preexistent figure, his divine mode of existence, his preexistent activity as agent of creation (in its pre-Gospel form the hymn went on to speak of the revelatory activity of the preexistent One in the world in general and in Israel's salvation history in particular). It also speaks, like the Philippians hymn, of the entry of the preexistent One into history: "the Word became flesh."[19] But there are differences. First, this hymn uses the title Logos; however, this is not significantly different from wisdom. Much more important is that it is the first time that the deity of the preexistent One is explicitly affirmed. "The Word was God." True, there is still a distinction between the deity of the preexistent One and the deity of God himself, for *theos* in verse 1c is anarthrous, and the Logos is still "with God," *pros ton theon;* turned toward God in a relation to him. Nevertheless, for the first time we encounter the word *theos* predicated of the preexistent One.

Now this Logos/Wisdom Christology is open to combination with other Christologies. The Logos incarnate is also the Son

(v. 14), and if we read "Son" rather than God in 1:18, "Son" can also be applied to the preexistent One. Throughout John's Gospel great prominence is given to the sending of the Son (cf. only John 3:17) into the world.[20]

It has frequently been pointed out that John's Gospel has no infancy narrative (although it makes one allusion to Jesus' birth in connection with the role he is to play in history, John 18:37). Jesus' mother figures twice in the Gospel, but there is no christological reflection on the significance of her giving birth to Jesus. It is often argued from this circumstance that the conception Christology of the Matthean and Lucan birth narratives and in the preexistence-incarnation Christology we have two fundamentally irreconcilable Christologies.[21]

Now, it is true that these particular Christologies are not combined by any New Testament writer.[22] But there are three considerations to be urged against the view that conception Christology and preexistence Christology are theologically irreconcilable.[23] First, we have noticed already a tendency within the New Testament for different Christologies to be combined: the Son of David and the sending-of-the-Son Christologies are combined in Rom. 1:3–4 and in the birth narratives of Matthew and Luke. The sending-of-the-Son and preexistence Christologies, both present though separated in the Pauline homologoumena, are combined in Hebrews and John. Second, the conception Christology of the birth narratives is, we argued, a dramatization of the sending-of-the-Son Christology. Thus we have a series of christological trajectories in the New Testament which are destined to converge. They may be represented diagrammatically thus:

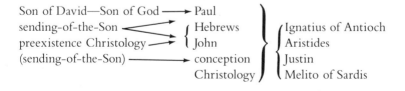

Third, our tracing of the conception Christology to its origin in the sending-of-the-Son pattern has revealed that the major difference between the two patterns is that in the conception Christology it is God who takes the initiative, whereas in the preexistence Christology it is wisdom who does so. Now, this is no novelty: we have here a difference which appears in the earthly stage Christology and in the postexistence Christology as well. In the earthly stage Christology we find the pattern "the Son was given up" (Rom. 4:25, reverential passive) on the one hand (cf. John 3:16), and "the Son of God who . . . gave himself up for me" (Gal. 3:20; cf. Eph. 5:2, 25). In the postexistence stage we find "God raised him (Jesus) from the dead" (Rom. 10:9) or "Christ was raised from the dead" (1 Cor. 15:4, reverential passive) and also the outspoken claim "I have power to lay (my life) down, and I have power to take it up again" (John 10:18). We touch here upon the deepest paradox of Jesus' earthly existence. His whole life was one of active obedience, and yet it was in and through that obedience that God performed his eschatological act. This paradox is extended to the preexistence and postexistence Christologies, because these Christologies interpret the ultimate significance of his history. Also, the presence of all these Christologies in what later became the canon of the New Testament indicates that the continuation of these trajectories past the New Testament is a legitimate, not an illegitimate, development. Our conclusion thus far is, therefore, that the New Testament points toward a development in which the origin of Jesus will be expressed in terms of the pneumatic-virginal conception of the preexistent One, who may be described in the ontic language of mythology as the preexistent wisdom being in the form of God, on an equality with God, the image of God, the preexistent Son, the reflection of God's glory, the very stamp of his nature, the Word who was with God, and finally in a carefully defined sense "God," though to be distinguished from God.

The Deity of Christ

Does the New Testament justify the calling of the incarnate One God? The nearest the synoptic Gospels come to this is in the

Matthean title, "Emmanuel." That, as we have seen, is not, however, to be interpreted ontically, but functionally and in terms of
salvation history. And it finds its fulfillment in the promise of the
exalted One (Matt. 28:20). The Pauline passages are much disputed. Romans 9:5 is the only passage in the Pauline homologoumena in which God is possibly used as a predicate for Christ:
"Christ, who is God over all, blessed forever" (RSV margin). But
doxologies in the Pauline homologoumena are normally addressed
to the Father (Gal. 1:5; Phil. 4:20; 2 Cor. 11:31; Rom. 1:25 and
11:36), and the RSV text is probably to be preferred: ". . . Christ.
God who is over all the blessed for ever." And even if it refers to
Christ, it is the exalted One. The same is probably true of other tex-
tually ambiguous passages, such as 2 Thess. 1:12, Titus 2:13, and
2 Peter 1:1. In all of these two-membered phrases, God and Christ
are probably meant to be taken as separate persons. And again, if
they do refer to Christ, it is to the exalted One.

In the Epistle to the Hebrews, the title *theos* originally applied
to Yahweh in Ps. 45:7 is transferred to the (exalted) Son (Heb. 1:8).
But in that same psalm verse there is a second occurrence of *theos*
which Hebrews retains for Yahweh; in other words, the exalted Son
of God, but with a difference. It is significant that this becomes
possible unequivocal predication of deity in a document which
expresses a wisdom Christology.

The same is true of the Fourth Gospel. There again the title
theos is predicated of the Son in his preexistent state (*theos ēn ho
logos*, 1:1) and as far as we have seen, less certainly in his incarnate
state as Revealer in John 1:18 (i.e., reading *monogenēs theos*),[24] but
quite certainly of the resurrected One in Thomas' confession
(*kyrios mou kai theos mou,* John 20:28). Finally, as a church confession we have *houtos* (sc. Jesus Christ) *estin ho alēthinos theos.* This
presumably refers to the preexistent, incarnate and exalted One. It
is significant that this occurs again in a stratum of the New Testament in which the wisdom Christology pattern is central. It was
the identification of Jesus as the incarnation of the divine wisdom
that made possible within the New Testament the eventual designation of Jesus as *theos.* But the wisdom Christology itself warns us
that it is not complete ontological identity. Jesus is identified as the

incarnation of God *in a certain aspect of his being:* in the being of God which is turned toward the cosmos, to humankind, to Israel, and to the church in revelatory and redemptive action. The later ontological Christology was careful to say that it was *God the Son* that became incarnate in the man Jesus, and precisely not God the Father. This is the limitation of the popular expression "God was made man," or that Jesus is God incarnate. We can say Jesus is God only with a particular nuance, a nuance that is derived from revelation in salvation history. Thus the wisdom Christology is on a trajectory which leads through the identification with the Son in a revelatory salvation-historical sense to an ontological Christology which affirms him to be God the Son.

The New Testament documents which affirm the deity of Christ in this particularly nuanced sense say nothing of his birth by Mary. The *theotokos* became possible only after the wisdom mythology of preexistence and incarnation was combined with the conception Christology of the birth narratives after the New Testament period. And the step was taken only when that mythological Christology was ontologically defined. But the *theotokos* undoubtedly stands at the end of a trajectory which is rooted in the New Testament. We may thus complete the trajectories which were diagrammed above thus:

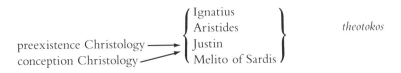

$$\begin{array}{l}\text{preexistence Christology} \longrightarrow \\ \text{conception Christology} \longrightarrow\end{array}\left\{\begin{array}{l}\text{Ignatius}\\\text{Aristides}\\\text{Justin}\\\text{Melito of Sardis}\end{array}\right\}\qquad \textit{theotokos}$$

Notes

1. For differing reasons, J. A. T. Robinson, F. Hahn, and the present writer have located the very earliest Christology in the kerygmatic speech of Acts 3:12–26, esp. vv. 13–15, 20–21. This is a "two-foci" Christology, looking backward on Jesus' historical career and forward to his consummation of all things as Son of man. See J. A. T. Robinson, "The Most Primitive Christology of All?" *JTS* NS 7 (1956): 177–89; repr. in *Twelve New Testament Studies* (SBT 34; London: SCM

Press, 1962), 139–53; F. Hahn, *Christologische Hobeitstitel* (FRLANT 83; Göttingen: Vandenhoeck & Ruprecht, 1963), 184–86. ET *The Titles of Jesus in Christology* (London: Lutterworth Press, 1969); R. H. Fuller, *The Foundations of New Testament Christology* (London: Lutterworth Press, 1965), 158–59.

2. For the functional and historical character of Hebraic-biblical thought, see G. Dix, *Jew and Greek* (Westminster: Dacre Press, 1953), 3–4; O. Cullmann, *The Christology of the New Testament* (Philadelphia: Westminster Press, 1959), 3–4.

3. On the wide acceptance of the pre-Pauline origin of this formula, see most recently M. Hengel, *The Son of God* (Philadelphia: Fortress Press, 1976), 59–60, and the bibliography there cited.

4. For the preference of "pattern" over "formula," the term previously used by W. Kramer, *Christ, Lord, Son of God* (SBT 50; London: SCM Press, and Allenson, Naperville, Ill., 1966), 186–89, see Hengel, *Son*. See also E. Schweizer, "Zum religionsgeschichtlichen Hintergrund der 'Sendungsformel,'" *ZNW* 57 (1966): 199–210, repr. in *Beiträge zur Theologie des Neuen Testaments* (Zürich: Zwingli Verlag, 1970), 83–95, esp. 90 n. 39. In the German the word used for pattern is "Schema."

5. The shift of opinion on this matter even with the Bultmann school has been remarkable. Until recently, his pupils generally agreed with him in finding the origin of preexistence Christology, including the sending-of-the-Son pattern, in the so-called pre-Christian gnostic redeemer myth. The latter theory was shattered by C. Colpe, *Die religionsgeschichtliche-Schule* (FRLANT 78; Göttingen: Vandenhoeck & Ruprecht, 1961). The alternative theory that the preexistence Christology, which is now gaining ground even within the Bultmann school, seems to have been first established by E. Schweizer in a series of articles. The earliest I have identified is: "Zur Herkunft der Präexistenzvorstellung bei Paulus," *EvT* 19 (1959): 65–70, repr. in *Neotestamentica* (Zürich: Zwingli Press, 1963), 105–9.

6. See esp. Schweizer, "Hintergrund," 84–90.

7. So Schweizer, "Hintergrund," 93, who thinks that the title "Son" penetrated the wisdom-sending-pattern from its earlier use in a prophetic context (Jesus as the culmination of the sending of the prophets, Mark 12:1–9).

8. See Fuller, *Foundations,* 231.

9. In a review of M. J. Suggs, *Christology and Law in Matthew's Gospel* (Cambridge: Harvard University Press, 1970); M. D. Johnson, "Reflections on a Wisdom Approach to Matthew's Christology," *CBQ*

36 (1974): 44–64, pointed out that the concept of sending is not characteristic of Jewish wisdom speculation. Rather, wisdom comes on her own initiative and seeks abode among the sons of men.

10. Its pre-Pauline origin is upheld by Kramer, *Christ, Lord, Son of God*, 115. Kramer further points out that the material from the formula fits awkwardly into Paul's sentence.

11. The most recent and thoroughly scholarly treatment of the infancy narratives is that of R. E. Brown, *The Birth of the Messiah* (Garden City, N.Y.: Doubleday & Co., 1977). See my review of this book in *CBQ* 40 (1979): 116–200.

12. See the comment by Brown, *Birth*, 152–53. Brown interprets Emmanuel to mean that in the coming of Jesus "the presence of God had made itself felt in an eschatological way." That affirmation, of course, is made in the light of the Christ event as a whole, upon which the early community looks back; the conception of Jesus marks the inauguration of the Christ event, but it is properly a prelude to the central aspect of the event—the ministry, life, death, and exaltation of the Christ.

13. Hahn, *Titles*, 260 and 275 n. 132, regards this verse at least as Lucan, though he thinks the visitation scene itself rests on pre-Lucan tradition. Brown, *Birth*, regards the whole scene as a Lucan composition.

14. See Brown, *Birth*, 517–33. Brown accounts for the conception Christology by a combination of two factors: (1) the historical fact that Mary became pregnant before the completion of her marriage with Joseph; (2) a successive retrojection of the Son of God Christology from the moment of resurrection/exaltation through the baptism to the conception. In my review of Brown's work in *CBQ* I observe that the basis for (1) is unfortunately tenuous. For (2) we propose as an alternative here that the conception Christology is a dramatization (modeled upon the annunciation patterns in the Old Testament) of the sending-of-the-Son Christology.

15. See the works by Schweizer, Hahn, and the present writer cited above. Cf. also J. M. Robinson and H. Koester, *Trajectories Through Early Christianity* (Philadelphia: Fortress Press, 1971), 232–68.

16. Schweizer, *Neotestamentica*, 106.

17. G. Bornkamm, "Zum Verständnis des Christus-Hymnus Phil. 2:6–11," in *Studien zu Antike und Urchristentum* (Ges. Aufs. I; BEvT 28; Munich: Kaiser, 1959) marshals the arguments for the pre-Pauline origin of the *Carmen Christi*. For a contrary view, see M. Hooker, "Philippians 2:6–11," in E. E. Ellis and E. Grässer, *Jesus und Paulus* (Kümmel Festschr.; Göttingen: Vandenhoeck & Ruprecht, 1975), 151–64.

18. For this interpretation of the much controverted word *harpagmos*, see E. Käsemann, "Kritische Analyse von Phil. 2:5–11," *ZTK* 47 (1950): 313–60. ET in R. W. Funk, ed., *God and Christ* (*JTC* 5; New York: Harper & Row, 1968), 45–88, esp. 63–65.

19. The Fourth Gospel uses the Logos hymn as an introduction to the baptism, not to the birth, for it has no birth narrative. See my article, "Christmas, Epiphany and the Johannine Prologue," in *Spirit and Light,* ed. W. B. Green and M. L'Engle (Edward West Festschr.; New York: Seabury Press, 1976), 63–73. I also argued that in the pre-Gospel form "the word became flesh" would have referred to the incarnate life in its entirety, not to any specific moment in it. But the parallel between *egeneto* and *genomenon* (Phil. 2:7) suggests now that we should include the birth as christological moment though, as in Philippians, only as the prelude to the total Christ event.

20. In my article "The Incarnation in Historical Perspective," in *Theology and Culture,* ed. W. T. Stevenson (C. L. Stanley and A. T. Mollegen Festschr.; *ATR* supp. series; Nov. 1976), I sought to show that this sending covers the whole earthly history of Jesus in its entirety. For the evangelist, the baptism of Jesus, with which the Gospel starts, is probably the initial moment of that sending. The birth, however, is a necessary prelude to that sending (cf. John 18:37).

21. So R. Bultmann, in *Kerygma and Mythos,* ed. H. W. Bartsch (*TF* 1; Hamburg: Reich & Heidrich, 1948), 24. ET *Kerygma and Myth* (London: SPCK, 1953), 11; J. A. T. Robinson, *The Human Face of God* (London: SCM Press, 1973), 50–66. R. Brown, *Birth,* is right in prescinding from the preexistence Christology in his exegesis of the birth narratives. What Matthew and Luke intended is not identical with what the later church discovered in these texts. When brought into relation with other writings within the canon, they acquire deeper meaning.

22. Brown, *Birth,* 141 n. 27, says this thought process was probably at work in Ignatius of Antioch. It is clearly expressed in Aristides, *Apol.* xv 1; Justin, *Apol.* xxxi and xxxiii; Melito of Sardis, *Discourse of Faith* 4.

23. I am not arguing for their harmonization as historical or suprahistorical events. Form-critically, the preexistence Christology is mythological and the conception Christology a legend. But the synthesized Christology explains inalienable truths about God and his self-disclosure in creation history, salvation history, and the Christ event.

24. Commentators are divided on the reading to be preferred here. R. Bultmann, *Das Evangelium des Johannes* Göttingen: Vandenhoeck & Ruprecht, 1956), 55–56 n. 4. ET *The Gospel of John* (Philadelphia: Westminster Press, 1971), 81–82 n. 2; C. K. Barrett, *The Gospel*

According to St. John (London: SPCK, 1955), 144, favor the reading *huion* on grounds of internal probability. But *theon* has the best MS support (the recently discovered p[66] and p[75] support it, as well as aleph and B). This reading is preferred by R. E. Brown, *The Gospel According to John* (AB 29; Garden City, N.Y.: Doubleday & Co., 1966), surprisingly by H. Conzelmann, *Grundriss der Theologie des Neuen Testaments* (Munich: Kaiser, 1968), 368. ET *An Outline of the Theology of the New Testament* (NTL; London: SCM Press, 1968), 337, and most recently by B. Lindars, *The Gospel of John* (NCB; London: Oliphants, 1972), 98. Opinion seems to be veering in favor of the reading *theon*. If so, it would be the only NT passage where *theos* is explicitly predicated of the incarnate One in his earthly life—a very important step along the trajectory to the *theotokos*.

PART FIVE

The Hellenistic Gentile Mission

7

JESUS CHRIST AS SAVIOR IN THE NEW TESTAMENT

The various versions of salvation in the New Testament have a prior unity in the event of the cross of Jesus Christ.

The Historical Jesus

The New Testament has many doctrines of salvation through Jesus Christ, but all of them tie this salvation to the cross. The cross, Bultmann has said, is the eschatological event par excellence.[1] But there were hundreds of crosses in first-century Palestine, and we may reasonably ask, What makes this particular cross the saving act of God? The answer might be, because only this cross was followed by a resurrection, or because only this cross is preached as the saving act of God in the kerygma. But in either case, faith in the saving efficacy of the cross looks suspiciously like an arbitrary imposition upon it, a myth in Bultmannian terminology, ideology in Schillebeeckx'. Only if the cross were related in some coherent way to Jesus' prior life, particularly to those two most certain elements in that prior life, his parables and his pre-Easter meals with his disciples and with the outcast, could it be otherwise. How can we relate these to the cross? At first sight the prospect is rather unpromising: the words of Jesus about his dying[2] are open to the suspicion of being, at least in their present form,[3] *vaticinia ex eventu*, and cannot therefore serve our purpose. But there is another, more helpful way to relate Jesus' eschatological proclamation and his meals to his dying. The traditions of the Last Supper, overlaid though the bread and cup words are with later liturgical accretion, contain three important sayings outside the bread and cup words. One is Jesus' saying about service. This has multiple attestation.[4] Here Jesus, in the context of a final meal, representing the climax of his previous meals, performs a solemn act of service to his disciples and relates it to his impending departure. He thus keeps up the posture of service to his own until his death. This gives a shape to the cross as an act of service. The second saying is the covenant saying which Luke gives independently of the cup word to which it was probably added through liturgical development: "I covenant (*diatithēmi*) to you a kingdom as my father has covenanted with me, that you may eat and drink at my table in my kingdom" (Luke 22:29–30). Here Jesus at the moment of his departure leaves a parting bequest, his kingdom.[5] This saying is wholly coherent with Jesus' pre-Easter eschatological proclamation. True, he has not used the word "covenant" before, but covenant and kingdom are intimately related.[6] The third saying is the "eschatological prospect." This enjoys double attestation (Mark, Special Luke), and is the most certain element in the Supper tradition.[7] Jesus asserts that he is now leaving the disciples: "I will no more eat/drink." But on the other side of that departure there is the certainty of the coming kingdom: "I eat/drink (my next meal) in my Father's kingdom." This saying, again, is coherent with Jesus' eschatological proclamation throughout his ministry.

These three sayings assure us that Jesus went to his death maintaining the same posture which had marked his entire ministry. The cross was the climax of his service for his friends: in going to the cross he bequeaths his kingdom to his disciples and assures them of the restoration of table fellowship with himself on the other side of his departure. Service, covenant, eschatological promise may all be interpreted as the offer of God's salvation.[8] Jesus' death is therefore not unrelated to his prior life, not an absurdity, like Camus' death on a motorcycle. His previous career gives meaning to the cross. Such a consideration saves the post-Easter kerygma of the cross from being myth or ideology.

Yet Jesus does not prescribe a doctrine of the cross. He does not hand out a theory of atonement on a plate. All such interpretations are post-Easter responses to the cross viewed through the prism of Easter. This applies even to those (rudimentary) interpretations of the cross provided in the bread and cup words of the Supper tradition. But if the reality of the cross lies in the attitude in which Jesus goes to it, then this is gain rather than loss. For it means that the variety of interpretations of the cross, even in the New Testament, all refer to one constant—the cross as Jesus' supreme offer of salvation to his own. We have prior unity in the event of the cross itself, quite independent of the diversity of interpretations which the NT traditions and authors offer after Easter.[9]

The Easter Event

The Easter event ("God raised Jesus from the dead"[10]) is integrally related to the cross as a salvation event: the cross's salvific quality resides inherently in itself. However, the Easter event is God's Yes to what Jesus stood for as he went to the cross. It says Yes: the whole life of Jesus, culminating in the cross, was indeed God's offer of salvation to the people, in face of the people's denial that it was so, registered in the rejection of Jesus' message and their sending him to the cross. Easter was the divine vindication of the salvific significance of Jesus' life, climaxed by the cross.

The Pre-Pauline Kerygmata

This No-Yes understanding of cross and Easter event (cross as Israel's No to God's offer of salvation; Easter event as God's Yes to it as indeed the offer of salvation) is the way the cross/resurrection are presented in the earliest kerygma as recorded in Acts: "This Jesus you crucified . . . God raised from the dead." It has often been noted that the christological formulae of this type contain no statement of the salvific significance of Jesus' death. They do not say that "Christ died for our sins" (1 Cor. 15:3). Yet if the argument here presented holds good, the No-Yes formula does indeed imply the salvific significance of the cross. Further, in the earliest kerygma the Easter event does not cancel out the cross. Rather, the Easter event makes the cross as salvific event ever available in the kerygma. There is truth in Willi Marxsen's formula *Die Sache Jesu geht weiter* (the cause of Jesus continues). But as a definition of the Easter event itself, it confuses cause with effect. The cause of Jesus continues after Good Friday only because God has raised Jesus from the dead and thus vindicated his cause. And his cause is precisely that he offered God's salvation.

If God had thus vindicated the crucified One, the exigencies of apologetic and catechesis demanded in a Palestinian environment that this rejection/vindication be demonstrably in conformity with the scriptures. As a result the cross itself, and not just Easter, was brought within the orbit of God's direct salvific action. The cross was not only Israel's rejection of the proffered salvation. It was itself part of the saving purpose of God. Christ also *died* according to the scriptures. The earliest community turned first to the psalms in order to make its case. For the psalms frequently follow the pattern of suffering/vindication. In particular, Psalms 22 and 69 were applied to the fate of Jesus, and the passion narrative was impregnated with the language of these psalms. Since the passion narrative was probably shaped as a Christian passover haggada to be recited at the passover feast as the exodus story was recited at the Jewish passover, this meant that the interpretation of the passion as "according to the scriptures" was taken up into the liturgy. It also found a place in the kerygma, as is indicated by the pre-Pauline kerygmatic formula in 1 Cor. 15:3, "Christ died . . . according to the scriptures."

It is surprising that the earliest Christians did not immediately utilize the servant songs of Deutero-Isaiah (including Isaiah 53). It seems to have taken them some time before they started using them, for they only slightly influenced the passion narratives and do not figure in the earliest forms of the kerygma. And even when they are pressed into use, there is a surprising absence of those verses which ascribe atoning significance to the servant's suffering (cf. Matt. 8:17 and Luke 22:37). When they first appropriated the servant texts, they were still operating within the framework of the No-Yes pattern of suffering/vindication. The evidence suggests that it was the requirements of the Christian paschal celebration that led the community eventually to take the momentous step of appropriating the atoning language of Isa. 53:10–11 for this purpose: "poured out," Mark 14:24 from Isa. 53:12;[11] "for" (hyper) Mark 14:24; 1 Cor. 11:24;[12] "many," Mark 14:24; 10:45;[13] "ransom," Mark 10:45.[14]

The fusion of the servant language with the covenant theme already present in the Supper tradition[15] led to the sacrificial interpretation of Christ's death. It was a covenant-inaugurating sacrifice, as the echo of Ex. 24:8 in the Marcan form of the cup word indicates. Paschal language appears also in the pre-Pauline formula, 1 Cor. 5:7. Both Palestinian-Aramaic-speaking Christianity after the Passover of A.D. 31 and Hellenistic-Jewish Christianity expressly interpreted Jesus' death as atoning and covenant inaugurating. Paul cites pre-Pauline formulae which confirm this. For instance, there is a formula in Rom. 3:24–26.[16] The death of Jesus is stated here to be an act of God. He initiates the whole process; it is not something done by the Son to change the Father's attitude. Jesus, for example, does not appease the wrath of God by his sacrifice. Rather, God in his mercy provided a way of forgiving sin by "putting forward" the Son.

This consideration predisposes us to reject the traditional translation "propitiation" for the much disputed word "hilastērion." For "propitiation" normally has man as subject and God as object; God's attitude is then changed from disfavor to forgiving love. Hence C. H. Dodd,[17] followed by many since (so RSV cf. NEB), argued for the translation "expiation," in which God is the subject and sin the object: What God in Christ has done is to remove sin as the obstacle to communion between God and the sinner. Not only does this conform to the LXX translation of KPR, meaning to "cover" or "cleanse," it also accords with the cross as a salvific act initiated by God.

Notwithstanding, there are scholars, particularly conservative evangelicals,[18] who while repudiating the notion that hilastērion implies a dichotomy of wills between the Father and the Son, and fully recognizing the divine initiative in the atonement, nevertheless retain "propitiation." Their argument is partly exegetical—in some passages, despite Dodd, *KPR* clearly means "propitiate."[19] It is also in part theological: "expiation" fails to do justice to the *wrath* of God. Unredeemed humanity stands guilty under his holy wrath. God, however, through his Son has propitiated his own wrath! Such a notion, absurd though it may seem, enshrines a profound truth, which alone does justice to the gravity of sin. We may applaud the theological concern here shown, but the weight of evidence favors "expiation." Perhaps the most balanced position is that of C. K. Barrett[20] who, while opting for expiation, recognizes that it has as it were the effect of propitiation.

However, wider theological considerations emerge when the pre-Pauline fragment is set in the context of Paul's argument in Romans. At the pre-Pauline level the meaning is undoubtedly "expiation," but at the level of the Pauline redaction it is moving in the direction of "propitiation." This should become clearer when we consider Paul's own doctrine of the cross.[21]

The word "blood," as we have seen, originates in the cup word at the eucharist. It does not denote simply "life," as has so often been asserted,[22] but *life which has passed through death*. It is therefore a sacrificial term.

The death of Christ is also an exhibition or demonstration of God's righteousness. In the past, God had apparently "passed over," or dealt lightly with sin, neither punishing it to the full as it deserved, nor removing it. Now, by giving up his Son to death, he has taken sin with full seriousness, not just forgiving it by a wave of the hand, but costingly, by the "blood" of his Son.

Another type of pre-Pauline soteriological formula is that which speaks of the sending of the Son. The pattern is: God as subject, followed by a verb of sending with the Son as object, and a purpose clause stating the soteriological intention. For examples see Gal. 4:4 and John 3:16.[23] The context in which both these formulae are cited is baptismal, and the *Sitz im Leben* of this type of formula would seem to be baptismal liturgy. The moment of the sending was probably identified with the Lord's baptism, when he became aware of his prophetic sending for his unique mission in salvation history. In time, however, the moment of sending was pushed back to his conception/birth as in the birth stories. Hence the statements of soteriological purpose in both the Matthean and Lukan birth stories (Matt. 1:21; Luke 1:68–69; 2:11).[24]

In pre-Pauline hymnody Christ's death and resurrection are also a triumph over the cosmic powers. Probably the earliest example is from the pre-Pauline hymn cited in Phil. 2:6–10 (see v. 10). The belief that the cosmos is under thrall of the powers of evil is apocalyptic, and the assertion of Christ's triumph over them is a natural development of the realized eschatology of the post-Easter community.

Paul and the Deutero-Pauline Literature

The theology of the cross was central both to Paul's initial kerygma and to the theology which, under pastoral necessity, he elaborated on the basis of it. He uses traditional sacrificial language in theological discussion but without elaborating, for example, "blood" for Christ's death as saving event (Rom. 5:9; 1 Cor. 11:27; cf. Col. 1:20). Wherever Paul uses the preposition "*hyper*" ("for") this comes from the pre-Pauline tradition of the cup word at the eucharist (Rom. 5:6, 8; 8:32; 14:15; 2 Cor. 5:15, 21; Gal. 1:4; 2:20; 3:13; 1 Thess. 5:10). Paul had emphasized the centrality of the cross in his initial preaching in Galatia (Gal. 3:1) and at Corinth (1 Cor. 1:23; 2:2). This does not mean that the resurrection played no part in his preaching. See the kerygmatic formula in 2 Cor. 15:3–4 and the explicit statement in verse 14. For Paul, as for the pre-Pauline kerygma, the Easter event does not cancel out the cross; it establishes and perpetuates its saving efficacy.

In the major letters Paul was dealing with four successive controversies, in each of which he responds with a theology of the cross. In Galatians and Romans he elaborates that doctrine in terms of justification by grace through faith (Galatians 3; Rom. 3:21–4:21). In First Corinthians he sets the folly of the cross over against human wisdom as a means of salvation. In Second Corinthians he sets forth the true understanding of apostleship as an epiphany of the cross in his sufferings.

Paul presents his doctrine of salvation under five major images: redemption, justification, reconciliation, victory, and sacrifice. All of these images, with the possible exception of reconciliation (which we have not encountered in the pre-Pauline material), come from earlier tradition. We will examine each of them in turn:

Redemption

With the discovery of the papyri it became customary to trace the origin of the image of redemption in the secular use for the manumission of slaves. There are, however, two sets of words for redemption. One set (*apolytrosis,* etc.) is applied in the Old Testament to the mighty acts of God in bringing Israel out of Egypt and making them his people (cf. Deut. 7:8; 1 Chron. 17:21) and in restoring Israel after the Babylonian captivity (Isa. 44:23). We have already encountered this word in Luke 1:68. Compare also Luke 21:28. It is therefore pre-Pauline. It probably first came from the vocabulary of the eschatological hope. It is a word of salvation history, not in the first instance a word for individual salvation. The relevant passages are Rom. 3:24; 8:10; Eph. 1:7, 14; 4:30; Col. 1:14. In Rom. 8:10 Paul characteristically uses two terms, *adoption* and *redemption*—which normally indicates what is already realized in Christian experience—for the ultimate eschatological hope. He never allows us to forget the elements of "not yet." In 1 Cor. 1:30 he includes redemption as one of the several meanings Christ has for the believers.

Paul has another word for redemption, *(ex)agorazō,* to "buy" or "buy back." It occurs in two contexts. In the first he emphasizes the *cost* of the redemption for God, the blood of his Son (1 Cor. 6:19–20; 7:23). The salvation-historical word, *apolytrōsis,* rooted as it was in the exodus and restoration from the exile, provided no opportunity to stress the cost of the redemption, so Paul also picked up *(ex)agorazō* from the contemporary social practice of the manumission of slaves. Since this is only an analogy, it would be wrong to press it (as later theology did both in connection with this word and the word *ransom* in Mark 10:45), by asking to whom the price or ransom was paid.

In the second context Paul uses *exagorazō* for redemption from the curse of the law (Gal. 3:13). What this curse is Paul has already stated in verse 10. He believes that no one has perfectly obeyed the law and so all humanity comes under that curse. God had to deliver us from that curse. This he did in the person of his Son by taking the curse upon himself. For he submitted to condemnation under the law and to death upon the cross, such a death involving a curse, according to Deut. 21:23 (Gal. 3:10). God in Christ thus absorbed into himself his own judgment upon sin, his own wrath. Here is the truth in the translation of *hilastērion* (Rom. 3:25) as propitiation rather than expiation. The importance Paul attached to redemption from the curse is signalized by his redaction of the sending-formula in Gal. 4:4 by adding "born under the law" and "to *redeem* those who are under the law."

Justification

We have already met this term in the pre-Pauline formula, Rom. 4:25. It also occurs in Luke-Acts (e.g., Luke 10:29; 16:15; 18:14; Acts 13:39), which shows that it is pre-Pauline. Paul, however, made it one of the key expressions of his theology, particularly in the Galatian and Roman controversies. The very contexts in which Paul elaborates this doctrine supports Krister Stendahl's[25] contention that justification must be interpreted not in terms of the Reformation's individualistic concern about the guilty conscience, but in terms of salvation history. Paul's problem was not that as a Jew he had a guilty conscience (Rom. 7:19 is not autobiographical), for as a Jew he had gloried in his own achievements (Gal. 1:14; Phil. 3:6), nor did Christ come as a solution to his personal problems. When he talks of justification by grace through faith apart from works of the law, he is responding to the concrete situations in Galatia and Rome, the admission of the Gentiles into the new covenant and the acceptance of Jews in a mixed community. This does not of course mean that the Reformation was wrong: it was wrestling with later problems created by the legacy of medieval piety, and it is arguable that its hermeneutic of Paul was faithful to the apostle, in changed circumstances. Once again, as

Martin Marty has observed, modern man has ceased to worry about the Reformation's problem, How can I find a gracious God? For Bultmann, modern man's problem was still individualistic, his inauthenticity—his bondage to the flesh, that is, his quest for security by his own strength. For the post-Bultmannian political theology, black theology, and liberation theology man's problems are social and cosmic.

Another problem related to justification has been the controversy over imparted versus imputed righteousness. Starting from the etymology of the verb *dikaioō* (cf. Lat. *iustificare*), Roman Catholic theology has understood it to mean "make righteous" in an ethical sense. The Reformation, on the other hand, interpreted justification in the light of the discussion in Rom. 4:6–12, according to which righteousness is imputed by a "legal fiction." The justified person was *simul iustus et peccator*. Today it is possible to get back behind the Roman Catholic/Reformation dilemma. Justification is essentially an eschatological act—God's verdict at the last judgment. In Christ this verdict is pronounced holy at their conversion/baptism in advance of the verdict pronounced proleptically; believers are thus brought into a right relationship with Christ at their conversion/baptism, which will be theirs at the end, and are empowered to grow in ethical righteousness, though there is still the tension between the already and the not yet. This also throws light on the pietistic distinction, unknown to Paul (1 Cor. 6:11), between justification and sanctification. The believers are pronounced upon them at the end, and this enables them to "become what they are" during this life.

Reconciliation

Paul also expresses salvation in Christ by the verb "reconcile," *katalessō*. It is this image that gave rise to the English term "atonement" (at-one-ment). The relevant passages are 2 Cor. 5:19; Rom. 5:10 (cf. Eph. 2:15, 16 and Col. 1:21, 22). Reconciliation is an image derived from warfare: God and mankind are viewed on opposite camps and need to be brought together ("at-oned") again. Humanity is in a state of rebellion, alienated and estranged from

God, his enemies (Rom. 5:6–11). God took the initiative in this situation (Rom. 5:6, 8). Once again, Paul is thinking in terms of Jews and Gentiles in salvation history, rather than of individuals. This reconciliation is accomplished *ante et extra nos* by the event of the cross. The preaching of the gospel is an announcement of an accomplished fact (2 Cor. 5:18–21). By accepting the message of reconciliation—that is, by conversion/baptism—the Gentiles proleptically appropriate the future eschatological gift of reconciliation and by becoming what they are experience the transformation of their hostility into glad and obedient service. Once again, the Reformation has universalized what Paul applied concretely to the admission of the Gentiles into the covenant and applied it to postmedieval humanity's quest for salvation from a guilty conscience. It thus went beyond Paul and asserted that God was reconciled to us (Article II). Again, this is a legitimate application, but it must be understood as a hermeneutical exposition, not an exegesis of what Paul meant. Once again, Bultmann and others have taken up and appropriated the concepts of alienation and estrangement in existentialist terms as the problem of inauthentic humanity, estranged from its true being. This too is hermeneutic, not exegesis.

Paul also utilized the victory language of his predecessors and extended the cosmic powers to include law, sin, and death. By his death Christ (or God in Christ) has delivered us from the law. Here law means way of salvation, not the enunciation of God's demand of obedience (Gal. 3:13). He has delivered us from the power of sin (Rom. 6:1–14) and from death (Rom. 8:2; 1 Cor. 15:20–28). Like other soteriological terms, the victory language preserves the tension between the *already* and the *not yet* (e.g., 1 Cor. 15:25).[26]

The Post-Pauline Writings

Hebrews

Hebrews is the only New Testament writing which has expounded Christ's death in terms of sacrifice. As we have seen, the *Sitz im Leben* of this image was the liturgy, and Paul had simply used it in traditional passages. Hebrews contrasts Christ's death sacrifice (the cross and entrance into the presence of God) with the Levitical sacrifices. At every point Christ's priesthood and sacrifice are superior and final. The author sees sin in terms of defilement, and the blood of Jesus as a cleansing from defilement.[27]

First Peter

First Peter reflects much paschal/baptismal language. Its soteriology is expressed mostly in traditional formulae enshrining sacrificial and victory language.[28] However, there is one passage which contains original reflection. This is in a paraenetic section (1 Peter 2:21–25). This passage echoes the soteriological language of Isaiah 53, but Christ's death is salvific because it is an example (v. 21).

The Johannine Literature

The Fourth Gospel appears to have gone through a number of stages before it reached its final form. At one stage, which I call narrative gospel (NG), a series of signs were combined with a passion narrative to demonstrate for non-Christian Jews that Jesus was the Messiah. This was achieved by the use of signs as direct proofs of his messiahship and by providing the passion narrative with Old Testament fulfillment quotations. In the next stage, the Revelation Gospel (RG), the narrative material was rearranged and the discourse material added. Experience had proved the inadequacy of the earlier demonstration approach. The signs are reinterpreted as pointers to the saving revelation brought by Jesus. What role does the passion play in RG? Is it retained, as some have held, simply as a concession to tradition, having no integral part in the evangelist's theology? It seems rather that everything promised in the revelation discourses becomes effective reality as a result of the cross. The cross releases the Paraklete, in which the revelatory/redemptive work of Jesus is made continually present in the life of the community. The final redactor of the Gospel, a close colleague, if not the same person as the author of First John, uses traditional soteriological language (cf. 1 John 1:7a) which had played only a minor role in RG. This has to do with his antidocetic purpose. He wishes to assert the reality of the flesh of Jesus, in which he truly became incarnate, suffered, died, and gives himself in the eucharist (John 6:51–59).

The Apocalypse may be a somewhat eccentric member of the Johannine community. It too enshrines much traditional soteriological language of liturgical provenance. For the Seer, Christ is the lamb slain from the foundation of the world (Rev. 5:6, etc.; cf. John 1:29, 36, which shows that this is traditional language of the Johannine community despite the different Greek words used for "lamb").

The Authority of Biblical Doctrines of Salvation Today

There are three major attitudes toward the Bible today: (1) the traditional view which regards the Bible as a direct source of authoritative doctrine; (2) the radical view for which the Bible is so irretrievably conditioned by its cultural settings that its message is irrelevant for modern man (on this view the most the Bible can do is to serve as one among many stimulating religious writings of the past[29]); (3) the mediating view that the Bible contains the saving message of God in Christ proclaimed through culturally conditioned language in the apostolic age.[30] On this view the message remains normative, the language and concepts through which it is proclaimed relative to the situation of the proclamation. Our questions are different from those of apostolic, patristic, medieval, and Reformation times. Hence the message of the Bible will speak differently to us from the way it spoke to Paul, Augustine, Anselm or Luther, and even to Bultmann. It is necessary for an initial distancing to recur, followed by a later fusion of the two horizons, that of the text and that of the interpreter. We opt for the third of these possibilities, not only as a *via media,* but because it seems sanctioned by scripture itself.

The soteriological data of the New Testament fall into three classes: (1) the actual Jesus event; (2) its proclamation and celebration in kerygma and liturgy; (3) the theological reflection of the

New Testament writers upon those data. The problem is how to relate the hermeneutical task to these three classes of data. Clearly, the Jesus event cannot itself be changed in any way: it happened, and happened in the original context of meaning given by Jesus himself. True, our access to it is only by way of critical sifting of data provided by materials impregnated with the post-Easter presentation of the happening in the data of class (2) and perhaps to a small degree of class (3). Our exhibition of the contextual situation in which the data of class (3) was shaped has shown that this material cannot today be simply repeated as it stands. What it says has to be translated into the contemporary context. The problem with class (3) material is whether and on what grounds this has an authority altogether different from postbiblical interpretation (e.g., from the soteriology of Augustine, Anselm and Luther, Calvin and Rashdall). In other words, we are confronted here by the problem of the canon. I hope to deal with this on a later occasion. But the real problem is with class (2) material. Do we have to take this as given data, commensurate with the original event itself, or does this too have to be "demythologized" or reinterpreted? Can we repeat "Christ died for our sins" and use it as basis for our theology as Paul, Hebrews, John, Augustine, Luther, and Calvin did? Or does even the basic kerygmatic assertion "Christ died for our sins" have to be restated? Has the uninterpreted kerygma binding authority? The New Testament answer seems to be yes in kerygmatic preaching and liturgy, but in paraklesis-preaching and theological reflection it must invariably be applied to the situation in hand. What "Christ died for our sins" means can only be understood in concrete situations. The New Testament message has basic authority. The application of that message for today has to be interpreted for the questions *we* ask.

Notes

1. Rudolf Bultmann, in *Kerygma and Myth,* ed. H. W. Bartsch (London: SPCK, 1972), 41.

2. Gerhard Kittel accepted the passion predictions as authentic ("Jesus Worte über sein Sterben," *Deutsche Theologie* [June 1936]: 175–82).

3. Edward Schillebeeckx thinks that the passion predictions, although *vaticinia ex eventu,* genuinely reflect the historical Jesus' attitude in his journey to Jerusalem (*Jesus* [New York: Seabury Press, 1979], 297f.).

4. Mark 10:42–45; Luke 22:24–27; John 13:1–20.

5. See Rudolf Otto, *The Kingdom of God and the Son of Man* (London: Lutterworth Press, 1943²), 271f.

6. Johannes Behm, "The *kainē diathēkē* is a correlative of the *basilia tou theou" (TDNT* 2:34).

7. Günther Bornkamm, *Jesus of Nazareth* (New York: Harper & Brothers, 1960), 160; Eduard Schweizer, *The Lord's Supper According to the New Testament* (Philadelphia: Fortress Press, 1967), 18–22.

8. Schillebeeckx speaks repeatedly of Jesus' eschatological message as the "proffer of God's salvation" (*Jesus*).

9. For J. M. Robinson, the cross is "Jesus' climatic (climactic?) actualization" of his eschatological message (*A New Quest of the Historical Jesus* [SBT 24; London: SCM Press, 1959], 89).

10. I suggested that it was the Christian passover celebration in A.D. 31 that gave rise to a backward-looking orientation of the eucharist to the death of Jesus ("The Double Origin of the Eucharist," *BibRes* 8 [1963]: 60–72). Norman Perrin was inclined to support this suggestion, but demurred at a date "as early as 31 C.E." (*A Modern Pilgrimage in New Testament Christology* [Philadelphia: Fortress Press, 1974], 76 n. 36). But why?

11. See Joachim Jeremias, *The Eucharistic Words of Jesus* (New York: Charles Scribner's Sons, 1966), 178.

12. Ibid., 179.

13. Ibid., 179–82.

14. In favor of a background in Isa. 53:11, 12: Ferdinand Hahn, *The Titles of Jesus in Christology* (London: Lutterworth Press, 1965); Perrin, *Pilgrimage* (p. 119) against C. K. Barrett, "The Background of Mark 10:45," in *New Testament Essays: Studies in Memory of T. W. Manson,* ed. A. J. B. Higgins (Manchester, Eng.: Manchester University Press, 1959); Morna Hooker, *Jesus and the Servant* (London: SPCK, 1959), 74–79; idem, *The Son of Man in Mark* (London: SPCK, 1967), 140–47.

15. See above.

16. For a reconstruction of the pre–Pauline hymn, removing Paul's glosses, see R. Bultmann, *Theology of the New Testament,* vol. 1 (London: SCM Press, 1952), 46.

17. C. H. Dodd, *The Bible and the Greeks* (London: Hodder & Stoughton, 1935), 82–95.

18. E.g., Leon L. Morris, "The Meaning of *hilastērion* in Romans iii.25," *NTS* 2 (1955): 33–43; idem, *The Apostolic Preaching of the Cross* (London: Tyndale Press, 1955), 125–85; G. E. Ladd, *A Theology of the New Testament* (Grand Rapids: Wm. B. Eerdmans, 1974), 429–33.

19. Zech. 7:2; 8:22; Mal. 1:9.

20. C. K. Barrett, *The Epistle to the Romans* (HNTC; New York: Harper & Brothers, 1957), 77f.

21. A third possible trans. of *hilastērion,* "mercy seat," has been suggested by Anders Nygren, and has found some support (*Commentary on Romans* [Philadelphia: Muhlenberg Press, 1949], 156–58). But in my opinion it has been decisively refuted by Eduard Lohse (*Märtyrer und Gottesknecht* [Göttingen: Vandenhoeck & Ruprecht, 1955], 150–52).

22. B. F. Westcott, *The Epistle to the Hebrews* (London: Macmillan & Co., 1889), 293–95.

23. The phrases referring to the law appear to be Pauline redaction. See Werner R. Kramer, *Christ, Lord, Son of God* (SBT 50; London: SCM Press, 1966), 112–14.

24. The older view that the *Benedictus* originated in "Baptist" circles has been rendered implausible by R. E. Brown, who argues for a post-Easter origin in a Christian community of *anawim,* those who had forsaken all to follow Christ (*The Birth of the Messiah* [Garden City, N.Y.: Doubleday & Co., 1977], 346–55).

25. Krister Stendahl, "Paul and the Introspective Conscience of the West," *HTR* 56 (1963): 199–215 repr. *Paul Among the Jews and Gentiles and Other Essays* (Philadelphia: Fortress Press, 1976), 78–96.

26. Space forbids treatment of the Pauline formula *en Christo.* See Fritz Neugebauer, who argues convincingly that it is salvation-historical and temporal rather than mystical and spatial (*In Christus* [Göttingen: Vandenhoeck & Ruprecht, 1961]).

27. See W. G. Johnsson, "Defilement and Purgation in the Book of Hebrews" (Vanderbilt Ph.D. thesis; Ann Arbor, University Microfilms, 1973).

28. Sacrificial language in 1 Peter 1:2; 2:21–24; 3:18. Victory language: 3:22; 4:6 (?).

29. D. E. Nineham, *The Use and Abuse of the Bible* (London: Macmillan & Co., 1976).

30. The views of the so-called new hermeneutic and of others brilliantly presented and discussed by A. C. Thiselton, *The Two Horizons* (Grand Rapids: Wm. B. Eerdmans, 1980).

8

EARLY CATHOLICISM

An Anglican Reaction to a German Debate

The presence of "early catholicism" in the New Testament was a German discovery. English-speaking scholarship debated a great deal over the authenticity of certain epistles of Paul and that of the Catholic Epistles, as well as over the reliability or otherwise of Luke-Acts. But even those scholars who took the more critical or radical line on these issues rarely drew full exegetical consequences from their recognition of the postapostolic dating of the works in question.[1] And those who maintained the conservative position usually ignored the question of early catholicism, at least so far as its presence in the New Testament was concerned.[2]

I agree that we have to accept that the Pastoral Epistles and Jude and 2 Peter are postapostolic (or perhaps it would be better to call them subapostolic), that they breathe a different atmosphere from the writings of the apostolic age. They also differ from the Gospels, which, though overlapping in part with the later writings in respect of chronology, preserve so much the earlier tradition of the apostolic age that they partly belong to it.

I agree also that the type of Christianity represented by these subapostolic documents is aptly described as early (or, as Norman Perrin has proposed, emergent) catholicism.[3] For it comprises a number of features which are more characteristic of the second century church than of the apostolic age. These features include an incipient canon of scripture, the replacement of the living voice of the kerygma with a more static concept of tradition, and a regularly ordained ministry.

If the English-speaking scholar is prepared to make these two concessions to German scholarship, the question arises, How is he to assess early catholicism? What authority should these writings have for the Christian church today? In the German debate, various answers have been proposed to this question. E. Käsemann favors the acceptance of a canon within the canon. Those writings which express the Pauline doctrine of justification by faith alone are to be fully normative of Christian faith and proclamation today, the other writings only insofar as they cohere with the message of justification.[4] But this involves a negative judgment on considerable portions of the New Testament, especially if we extend our list of early catholic writings to include Luke-Acts and the deutero-Pauline Colossians and Ephesians. It is, therefore, not surprising that systematic theologians especially have been unhappy with this. H. Diem, for instance, opts for conservative authorships and datings of the writings in question, and adopts an exegesis of them that makes them apostolic rather than early catholic.[5] This line would be followed by a considerable number of English-speaking writers. W. Marxsen in turn seeks to relativize the early catholic writings by explaining them in situational terms. They were a response to early gnosticism, a situation allegedly no longer obtaining, and are therefore no longer normative (at least in their early catholic aspects) to the church today.[6] A quite different point of view was put forward by the Roman Catholic systematician H. Küng. While agreeing with the later datings of this body of literature and recognizing their early catholic character, he argued that early catholicism pointed beyond itself to later catholicism, which thus acquired canonical justification as a natural development.[7] How does an English-speaking Anglican react to this (mainly) German debate?

There is undeniable difference of atmosphere and of priorities between the apostolic and the subapostolic age. These differences cannot be ironed out by conservative datings and harmonizing

exegesis. Further, such features as an organized, regularly constituted and ordained ministry, a crystallization of Christian faith in
the form of tradition, the incipient canon of scripture which begins to emerge in this period would seem to merit the designation
of early or emergent catholicism. The real problem in an assessment of the legitimacy of these developments is whether there are
significant elements of continuity as well as of discontinuity between the two epochs. German scholarship has tended to empha-
size the discontinuity. The problem is analogous to the question
of the relation of the proclamation of the historical Jesus to the
post-Easter church. In the early period of form criticism there
was an overemphasis on the discontinuity here, and it was not until the so-called new quest of the historical Jesus that sufficient attention was paid to the significant elements of continuity between
the two phases, Jesus and the post-Easter church. Similarly, Käsemann, Marxsen, and others have arguably overemphasized the
discontinuity (which is certainly present and must be recognized)
and underestimated the elements of continuity between the apostolic age and early catholicism.

The elements of discontinuity are patent enough. The eschatological tension between the already and not yet is relaxed in
favor of an almost exclusive (though probably never complete) concentration on the already, on realized eschatology; or else the final
consummation is postponed to such an indefinite future as to deprive eschatology of immediate existential relevance. The free,
charismatic type of ministry in the Pauline churches as evidenced
in 1 Corinthians 12 and Romans 12 is replaced by the ordered
ministry of the Pastorals. The concern for the living voice of the
kerygma, manifested, for example, in 1 Thess. 1:9; 1 Corinthians
1–3, and Rom. 1:16–17, is replaced by a concern for the maintenance of the deposit (παραθήκη) in the Pastorals.

The question of continuity versus discontinuity will have to
be decided by the following criteria:

1. The new elements emerging in the subapostolic age must
    be shown to be present, latently at least, and *mutatis mu-
    tandis,* in the apostolic age.

2. When they emerge they must demonstrably not suppress the concerns of the apostolic age, but serve the continuity of those concerns.

We shall now try to apply these two criteria to three of the main features of early catholicism: the canon of the New Testament, the deposit of faith, and the development of the regularly constituted ministry.

The Canon of the New Testament

No one, so far as I can see, has seriously questioned the legitimacy of a canon of scripture. Yet this is precisely one of those institutional features that emerged with early catholicism. The real problem has been not the canon in and of itself, but the limits of the canon. Are the later books in which the presence of early catholicism has been detected part of the norm of Christian faith and practice, or are they merely sources for the history of the subapostolic age?

In answer to that question, it needs to be noted that our present-day situation is in important respects more analogous to that of the subapostolic age and early catholicism than it is to the apostolic age. We, too, are postapostolic, and therefore also epigoni, no longer primary sources of witness to the Christ event. We, like them, have to derive our Christian truth from the original witnesses of the Christ event. Thus the New Testament documents of the early catholic period can be helpful to the present-day church because they show that the generation which immediately followed the apostles had to cope with the same basic problem which is ours; namely, how to remain apostolic in faith and practice now that the original witnesses are removed from the scene; or to put it in other words, how to maintain Christian identity in an age of derived witness. In order to cope with this problem, the church of the subapostolic age collected and used as norms the writings which emanated from the apostolic age, such as the incipient Pauline corpus and the Gospels. It is surely an advantage that the canon itself contains at least one document (2 Peter) which both recognizes the need for such a canon and which at the same time bears witness to its formation. The principle of canon is recognized in the canon itself! For this reason alone we would question the appropriateness of Käsemann's outburst, "What have we to say about the canon in which 2 Peter has a place as the clearest possible testimony to the onset of early catholicism?"

There are other ways in which our age is more like that of the subapostolic period than it is like the apostolic age. We, too, have to adjust to the delay of the *parousia*. It is doubtful whether we can realistically maintain the Pauline tension between the already and the not yet at the same pitch as the apostle did in the face of the *parousia's* nonarrival two thousand years after. The various answers that the early catholic writers produced in face of that challenge—a shift of emphasis to the already, coupled with the maintenance of the hope of an ultimate consummation, the recognition that God's time scale transcends our own—are not without relevance to our situation today.

We, too, have to realize that the church is here to stay, that it has to settle down and live in this world. If we had only the Jesus tradition as enshrined in the synoptic Gospels and the Pauline homologoumena, we might be tempted to a pietistic neglect of the claims of this present, a pietism which would be ultimately false to the proclamation of Jesus and to the kerygma of the post-Easter church. The household codes, for instance, warn us that we must take seriously the continued existence of the church in the world and the claims of human society. As L. Goppelt has observed, the whole point of the household codes is to teach "verantwortliches Bleiben in den Institutionen." They are directed against "emigration" more than "rebellion."[8]

During the Barthian period there was much debate on whether or not there was such a thing as natural theology. The more important question would be the desirability of a theology of the natural order. We must take seriously today the cultural tasks of the church. We must take seriously the quest for God in the non-Christian religions. It is precisely the early catholic writings of the New Testament that provide us with the resources for these present-day theological tasks. Consequently, we should rejoice that the canon of the New Testament contains these writings, and we should not in effect reduce our canon so as to ignore them in our proclamation and practice. This concern for the natural order is, be it noted, not a novelty of the subapostolic age. It is not a falsification of Jesus' proclamation or of the post-Easter message. Jesus' parables assume the reality and the dignity of the created order. Paul, and not only the deutero-Pauline Ephesians, accorded human marriage the dignity of being a parable of the ultimate relationship between Christ and his church (2 Cor. 11:2). Jesus and Paul were thus as much opposed to "emigration" as were the household codes. But with Jesus and Paul these concerns were uttered in a whisper that was likely to be drowned out by the much louder tones of their proclamation of the kingdom and of Christ crucified, and of his imminent coming, respectively. Thus, on the question of the natural order there is continuity as well as discontinuity between Jesus and the apostolic age and early catholicism. But precisely because this discontinuity lies in the shift from implicit assumption to explicit assertion, we can profit by the early catholic writings as models for the preservation of the values of the apostolic age in a postapostolic church.

The Deposit of Faith

Preaching Christ crucified and the imminent *parousia* with Paul is, of course, much more exciting than guarding the deposit with the author of the Pastorals. But, as the subapostolic writers realized in face of the growing challenge of gnosticism, the only way to continue faithfully to preach the apostolic message was by means of the control of the apostolic tradition. One cannot really argue, as Marxsen has done, that this was a temporary emergency now long past.[9] True, it is not exactly the same challenge that the Christian church has to face today as the first- and second-century churches had to face with gnosticism in their day. But a century which has known the successive challenges of Kultur-Prostestantismus (and Kultur-Katholizismus in Northern Ireland), National Socialist ideology, atheistic Marxism, secular humanism, and the like, cannot dismiss the concern to maintain the deposit of faith in the form of the creed and confession as irrelevant. Of course, mere preservationism is not enough. A deposit is like food put into the deep freezer. It has to be taken out and thawed if it is to be used. But if the housewife goes to the freezer and finds nothing there, she won't have anything to cook for dinner. A church which has no deposit of faith has no resources to draw upon in time of need.

Naturally, as H. Küng and also K. Schelke (who similarly recognizes the presence of early catholicism in the New Testament) have reminded us, the early catholic writings make no claim to be the whole of the New Testament.[10] They exist in a canon which also contains Pauline homologoumena and the synoptic Gospels, a fact to which 2 Peter explicitly calls attention. Hence these writings point away from themselves to the earlier and primary documents of the New Testament, and so invite judgment upon themselves in the light of their predecessors.

H. Küng has pointed a finger of accusation to his own ecclesiastical tradition, charging it with *haeresis* in the literal sense, selectivity in its deference to the New Testament.[11] Whereas the Reformation churches tended to base their proclamation too exclusively on the Pauline homologoumena, the Roman Catholic Church has, he claims, paid excessive deference to Pastorals and 2 Peter. He therefore pleads for an adherence to the whole canon as opposed to à la carte selection, raising the demand for "evangelical concentration and catholic comprehensiveness." His warning should be taken seriously by the heirs of conservative Reformation. These churches (Lutheran, Anglican, and Reformed) after all did, broadly speaking, retain many of the features of early catholicism (including creed and confessions). These features have to be seen as deriving their meaning and importance from the way in which they serve the primary concern of the New Testament message.

They must not be seen as ends in themselves (as Rome has done) nor as dispensable impediments.

A Regularly Constituted Ministry

Eduard Schweizer, in whose honor this essay is written, has, together with other German-speaking scholars such as E. Käsemann and H. von Campenhausen, devoted much thought to the origins of the church's ministry.[12] They have made it abundantly clear that in the Pauline congregations, at least, the ministry was of a free charismatic type. The Spirit welled up within the congregation and created such ministries as were required on an *ad hoc* basis. Käsemann goes so far as to suggest that this is the only type of ministry compatible with the Pauline *theologia crucis*.[13] The institutionalization of the ministry, as in the Pastorals, is thus seen not only as a declension from the apostolic age, but as a corruption. This, however, is to overlook the presence of the all-important factor of the primary witnesses in the apostolic age. As long as these primary witnesses were present, whether physically or, as often in the case of Paul, by means of an epistle, the free charismata could be kept subservient to the gospel. Indeed, the very existence of 1 Corinthians is the supreme witness against the free-for-all notion of the charismata. The whole energy of Paul's epistolary activity is there directed against the uncontrolled exercise of the charismata. Thus the apostle lays controls on the charismatics and sets down rules for the exercise of the charismata (1 Corinthians 12–14). He further makes doctrinal and ethical decisions (e.g., 1 Cor. 7:39–40; 11:7–34). He does this despite the fact that he recognizes that all the members of the body have their charismata. They must confess Jesus as Lord (1 Cor. 12:3). This element of apostolic control is perpetuated in the Pastorals through the institution of bishop/presbyters under "Timothy" and "Titus." This is not the introduction of something wholly new, but the preservation of an element in the total picture that was already present in the apostolic age. Of course, it is true that in the process the charismatic ministries were allowed to wither away. To that extent there was a real loss. But that loss is not something which is integral to the developed system itself. Even 2 Peter appears to recognize that the Spirit is not a monopoly of a special class of ministers, but is present in the congregation as a whole.[14] What is wrong in all of the mainline churches is not ordination and ministerial succession as such. These are instruments for the continuation of the apostolic gospel from generation to generation. What is wrong is their isolation from the Spirit-bearing body as a whole.

The New Testament, of course, does not prescribe in a legalistic way what the precise structure of ministry and church office should be. In fact, the New Testament writings represent a cutoff at a certain stage of development. This development received a classic form in the second century, by which time most congregations had a ministry consisting of a bishop with presbyters and deacons. Yet the development did not stop there. The original corporate presbyterate over which the Ignatian type of bishop presided as *primus inter pares* was broken up in both East and West in the development of the diocese in response to the needs of missionary expansion. In the East there was the further development of the patriarchate and in the West the development of the papacy (later claiming first universal jurisdiction and finally infallibility). When the churches of the Reformation shook off the papal yoke, they either reverted to some more primitive form of episcopacy, or evolved new forms of synodic or presbyterial order, or adopted the principle of congregationalism. Only in the case of the Quakers and Pentecostalist bodies there has been a revival of the free charismatic type of ministry manifested in the Pauline homologoumena, though without the apostolic control that those documents presuppose. None of these later developments have direct sanction from the New Testament. They have to be judged by the same criteria by which we assessed the developments of early catholicism in the New Testament. Do they maintain continuity with the earlier periods covered by the New Testament? Are the new elements which they feature somehow latent or implicit in the earlier periods? Do they serve as means of preserving the essential message of the gospel, or do they become ends in themselves, so that they obscure or stifle that message?

Conclusion

As an Anglican looks at the developments of early catholicism in the New Testament and reviews the German debate to which [Eduard Schweizer] has contributed significantly, he need feel no qualm about those elements that are distinctive of his church's position (canon, creed, and historical episcopate). They all have implicit sanction in the New Testament. They are not in and of themselves illegitimate developments. They need not be a threat to or a denial of the essential message of the gospel. They are meant to be safeguards of that gospel, deriving solely from it. But at the same time, the Anglican must listen to the warning of J. Knox when he drew a distinction between the authority of the central message of the New Testament and that of the early catholic developments:

> The Catholic must also be ready to acknowledge the soundness of the historic Protestant emphasis upon a distinction as regards normative value between the "first century" and any later century. Something essential is lost if one reduces the authority of the first century to the level of the second, or (which is the same thing), raises the authority of the second to the level of the first. The ultimate norm in Christianity is the event of which the primitive church is the immediate reflection; the essential being of the church, in the qualitative or concrete sense as the new community of the Spirit of Christ, was given in that event.[15]

But there is also the opposite warning of another Anglican, Bishop Stephen Neill, who pleaded that what J. Knox called the second century and what we have been speaking of as early catholicism had a necessary though subordinate place:

> "The faith" may be less exciting than "faith." Yet it may be a necessary element in conserving, if not creating, the image of Jesus Christ among men, and holding the fort until the time for new creative discovery has come. The pastoral Epistles do not make the same contribution as the Epistle to

the Romans; yet it may be recognized that they too serve a legitimate and Christian purpose.[16]

Notes

1. An exception is J. D. G. Dunn, *Unity and Diversity in the New Testament* (Philadelphia: Westminster, 1977), esp. 341–66. His concern with early catholicism is mainly phenomenological, rather than systematic.

2. A conservative evangelical scholar like G. E. Ladd can treat the Pastorals (as well as Ephesians) as Pauline and 2 Peter as Petrine without argument, subsuming their early catholic features into the overall picture of the apostolic age. See G. E. Ladd, *A Theology of the New Testament* (Grand Rapids: Wm. B. Eerdmans, 1974), 530–37, 602–7.

3. N. Perrin, *The New Testament: An Introduction* (New York 1974), 61.

4. E. Käsemann, *Essays on New Testament Themes* (London: SCM Press, 1964), 95–107. ET of "Begründet der neutestamentliche Kanon die Einheit der Kirche?" first published in *EvT* 11 (1951/52): 13–21.

5. H. Diem, *Dogmatics* (London 1959), 109–204, 229–34. ET of *Dogmatik: Ihr Weg zwischen Historismus und Existentialismus* (München 1955).

6. W. Marxsen, *Der "Frühkatholizismus" im Neuen Testament* (Neukirchen 1958), 69–70.

7. H. Küng, "'Early Catholicism' in the New Testament as a Problem in Controversial Theology," in *The Living Church: Reflections on the Second Vatican Council* (London 1963), 223–93.

8. L. Goppelt, *Theologie des Neuen Testaments,* vol. 2 (Göttingen 1976), 497.

9. Käsemann, *Essays,* 195 = "Eine Apologie der urchristlichen Eschatologie," *ZTK* 49 (1952): 272–96.

10. Küng, "Early Catholicism," 28; K. Schelke, "Frühkatholizismus," *LTK,* ²1964.

11. Küng, "Early Catholicism," 284–87.

12. E. Schweizer, *Church Order in the New Testament* (SBT 32; London 1961); Käsemann, *Essays,* 63–94 = "Amt und Gemeinde im Neuen Testament," in *Exegetische Versuche und Besinnungen* (Göttingen ⁶1970), 109–33; H. von Campenhausen, *Ecclesiastical Authority and Spiritual Power in the Church in the First Three Centuries* (Stanford, Calif.,

1969) = *Kirchliches Amt und geistliche Vollmacht in den ersten drei Jahrhun-derten* (Tübingen 1953).

13. Käsemann, *Essays,* 92. Such a claim is calculated to stifle all serious debate of a subject on its own merits, for it is incapable of proof or refutation.

14. See 2 Peter 1:1b, which suggests that ministers and people are of equal standing so far as their salvation is concerned, and 1:12, which says that the addressees are established in the truth, so that truth is not a clerical monopoly.

15. J. Knox, *The Early Church and the Coming Great Church* (New York/Nashville: Abingdon Press, 1955), 146. Note that Knox places "first century" in quotation marks. It stands for apostolic Christianity as opposed to "early catholicism."

16. Neill does not use the term "early catholicism," but that is what he is talking about. It is interesting that he heads this chapter of his work "A Response to a Response." That is exactly what early catholicism is in relation to the apostolic message, which in turn is a response to the Christ event.

PART SIX

The Post-Easter Church

CHAPTER

9

PREEXISTENCE CHRISTOLOGY: CAN WE DISPENSE WITH IT?

In precritical times there was no problem with preexistence Christology. It had its sanction in the teaching of Jesus as recorded in the Fourth Gospel (e.g., John 8:58; 10:30; 13:3; 17:5). Now that we cannot employ the discourse material of the Fourth Gospel as direct evidence for the *ipsissima verba* of Jesus, some have sought to find sanction for it in Jesus' use of Son of man as a self-designation. However, even if we grant that the title "Son of man" was already fixed in pre-Christian Jewish apocalyptic for a preexistent figure to be manifested as eschatological judge and savior, and even if we grant that Jesus did use the term and use it as a self-designation—all of which is greatly in dispute[1]—there is no indication anywhere in the synoptic Son of man sayings of the Son of man's preexistence.

Indeed, there is fairly wide consensus today that the preexistence Christology is a post-Easter development. When exactly this development took place is not clear. Those who regard Phil. 2:6–11 as a pre-Pauline hymn, and who interpret verses 6–7 as referring to a preexistent state, would date this development between A.D. 35 and 50 (so M. Hengel[2]). Those who interpret the Philippian hymn in terms of a two-stage Christology—involving only earthly life and postexistence[3]—would find the earliest occurrence of preexistence Christology in 1 Corinthians (esp. 1 Cor. 8:6). Thereafter it is found in hymnic materials both within the Pauline school (Col. 1:15–20) and beyond it (Heb. 1:3–4), in the Johannine prologue and (see the references above) in the discourse material of that Gospel.

Hans Grass and others have argued that contemporary systematic theology should abandon preexistence Christology.[4] It is, they say, irretrievably mythological. It has no basis in the self-understanding of the historical Jesus. It was unknown in the earliest kerygma, which focused rather on the death and exaltation of Jesus. When it does appear it is confined almost entirely to hymnic materials, and until the Fourth Gospel little attempt is made to integrate it into the theology of those writings where it appears. When used today, it shifts the focus of Christology away from the death and resurrection of Jesus, where the focus properly belongs. It distorts the picture of Jesus as he really was, a truly human person, making him instead a celestial visitor from an alien world.

Grass asks whether preexistence and incarnational Christology is the only way to express the significance (*Bedeutsamkeit*) of Jesus for faith. A "sending" Christology should be sufficient, a Christology which speaks of Jesus' historical mission. Such a Christology would safeguard the divine initiative behind the history of Jesus, and the presence of God in him. It would allow for a distinction between the sending of Jesus and the sending of the prophets, for it would recognize that the sending of Jesus was definitive, permanent, and universal in significance. It would speak of preexistence but in an "ideal" sense, not of a real, substantial, or personal preexistence. It would speak of the election of Jesus of Nazareth from all eternity to be the medium of God's final revelatory and saving act.

Such an interpretation is particularly attractive, since it is no mere reversion to the older liberal Christology in which Jesus had the value of God for us because of the sublimity of his teaching and human personality. Moreover, it allows for a God who acts, for human sin, and for finality of God's redemption in Jesus Christ. On the other hand, it involves the abandonment not only of the incarnation as traditionally understood but also, as Grass himself notes, the doctrine of the Trinity. The question is whether this substitution of a "God in Christ" Christology for traditional Christology does justice to the biblical witness.

Let us try to deal in turn with the objections to the preexistence Christology presented above. The first objection is that it is mythological. This objection originates in part from the theory that the preexistence Christology was an importation from pre-Christian gnosis in the shape of the so-called gnostic redeemer myth. This theory, originating in the History of Religions School, enjoyed a long popularity, especially among the Bultmannians, but was conclusively demolished by C. Colpe in 1961.[5] The publication of the Nag Hammadi documents more recently has not materially altered the situation.[6] A series of articles by E. Schweizer from 1959 on[7] has created a widespread consensus that the source of preexistence Christology is to be found in the Jewish speculation about the divine Wisdom. Is this speculation correctly characterized as mythological? It would be if Wisdom were an actual being, somehow distinct from the being of God. But recently, J. D. G. Dunn has argued persuasively that Wisdom in this speculation is no more than a personification of a certain aspect of God's activity: "Wisdom never became more than a convenient way of speaking about God acting in creation, revelation, and salvation; Wisdom never became more than a personification of God's own activity."[8] If this is so, then the identification of Jesus with God's Wisdom does not involve the mythological idea of a preexistent divine being, in some way distinguishable from the being of God, becoming incarnate. What it is saying is that that aspect of the being of God which Jewish thinkers had previously experienced has become now fully embodied in the life of Jesus. There is really nothing mythological about this.

Does all this have any basis in the self-understanding of the earthly Jesus? Since the pursuit of the so-called New Quest, it has usually been held that Jesus' eschatological message, his conduct, and so forth, all "implied a Christology," or they were an assertion of an "indirect Christology." We have no intention of quarreling with that claim, and in fact we have frequently advanced it ourselves. We would, however, for present purposes propose a substitute. What this really means is that Jesus held what E. Schillebeeckx has called in a slightly different connection (viz., with reference to the kerygma of the earliest post-Easter community) a "theology of Jesus."[9] That is to say, Jesus spoke and acted, even if he did not explicitly assert it in so many words, that God was present speaking and acting through him. In fact, E. Fuchs, one of the proponents of an "implied Christology," actually formulates this in terms of Jesus' "daring to speak and act for God" (this in reference to his conduct in eating with the outcast).[10]

Now this is a far cry from a preexistence Christology, and in fact at first sight it seems rather to support H. Grass's proposed substitution "God was in Jesus." Yet, as Jesus' eschatological proclamation shows, he regarded his activity as the eschatological culmination of God's dealings with his people. The same God was present in him as had been present throughout Israel's history.[11] Here we have the basis upon which the later preexistence Christology was to develop.

Nor was this view of Jesus unknown to the earliest kerygma.[12] True, the earliest kerygma had no preexistence Christology. Indeed, the earliest Christology is often characterized (see, e.g., Acts 2:36 and Rom. 1:3) as "adoptionist." A closer examination of it, however, indicates that the earliest community continued precisely Jesus' own "theology of Jesus" so far as the interpretation of his earthly life was concerned. In fact, we might describe the earliest Christology as a "theology of Jesus" interpretation of his earthly life combined with an explicit Christology for his postexaltation existence:

> Jesus of Nazareth, a man attested to you by God with mighty works and wonders and signs *which God did through him* in your midst (Acts 2:22).
>
> He went about doing good and healing all that were oppressed by the devil, *for God was with him* (Acts 10:38).

Indeed, we might regard the famous Pauline statement "In Christ God was reconciling the world to himself" (2 Cor. 5:19) as a survival of the primitive "theology of Jesus," a theology Paul can still use after he has accepted an explicit Christology for the earthly life of Jesus, and (what is perhaps even more significant) at a time when he has already used hymnic materials affirming preexistence Christology.

It is perfectly true, as Grass has observed, that even after the introduction of preexistence Christology it remains, until the Fourth Gospel, rather peripheral. It is confined almost exclusively to hymns, although where these hymns are quoted the preexistence part of it cannot be dismissed as irrelevant to the theological argumentation. In Philippians (if the hymn does indeed feature preexistence) it serves to reinforce the exhortation to humility. In 1 Corinthians the portrayal of Jesus as the embodiment of Wisdom serves to counter the false notions of Wisdom prevailing at Corinth. In Colossians the attribution of creation to the preexistent One serves to counter the Colossians' ascription of creation to the angelic powers, thus introducing a dualism which undermined the kerygma by denying the salvability of creation.[13] At the same time we must admit, however, that no effort is made by the New Testament authors until the Fourth Gospel to integrate the preexistence Christology to the rest of their Christology.

As for the next objection—that a preexistence Christology shifts the focus away from the death and resurrection of Jesus where it really belongs—this may be true of some Christologies in the post–New Testament period, but it is not true of the New Testament (not even, I would argue, *pace* Bultmann, of the Fourth Gospel) nor of the concern of the classical christological definitions,[14] nor of the Reformation Confessions.[15] Treated rightly, therefore, the preexistence and incarnation Christology provides the indispensable basis for the right understanding of the cross and resurrection.

The last objection to the preexistence and incarnational Christology is that it distorts the picture of Jesus as he really was, a truly human being and not a celestial visitor from an alien world. Now this Christology never asserts in mythological fashion that the man Jesus was preexistent. The statements about preexistence refer not to Jesus in himself, but to Wisdom, that is, that aspect of the being of God which was incarnated in Jesus. True, in some hymnic passages the antecedent of "who" is "Jesus Christ" (Phil. 2:6;

1 Cor. 8:6). But these passages do not have as their antecedent simply "Jesus," and therefore I would argue that the relative clauses
have as their antecedent Jesus in his revelatory and salvific capacity.
Strictly speaking, the relative clauses speak of "that of God which is
incarnated in the man Jesus."[16] Since therefore it is not Jesus as such
who is thought of as preexistent, and since Wisdom is not a personal mythological being, but an aspect of the being of God, it
follows that the preexistence Christology is not mythological, and
that therefore it cannot have the effect of making Jesus a celestial
visitor from an alien world.

If this is the true interpretation of that Christology, have we
not purchased our solution at the cost of surrendering any real
Christology? Does it not leave us after all merely with a theology of
Jesus? Is not Grass finally right, and can we not simply content
ourselves with the assertion that "God was in Christ"? Now the
Fourth Gospel goes beyond this. It alone, of all the New Testament
writings, has sought to integrate the Wisdom Christology with the
earthly life of Jesus. More specifically, it has integrated the Christology of the incarnation of the divine Wisdom (or Logos, to use the
language of the Prologue, though that language is not picked up in
the rest of the Gospel) with a Christology of the Father and the Son:

> The Father loves the Son, and has given all things into his
> hand (John 3:35).
>
> The Son can do nothing of his own accord, but only what he
> sees the Father doing; for whatever he does, the Son does
> likewise. For the Father loves the Son, and shows him all
> that he himself is doing (John 5:19–20).

This Father-Son language is not pure speculation, but is rooted in
the undoubtedly historical fact of what Schillebeeckx calls Jesus'
Abba experience. The Johannine writer would claim that this development is the result of a prolonged meditation on that experience under the guidance of the Paraclete (or Counselor), whose
function is "to take what is mine and declare it to you" (16:14).
On one level this Father-Son Christology is an exposition of the
earthly experience of the man Jesus. But because Jesus is the earthly

manifestation of the divine Wisdom or Logos, his life is a disclosure of a mutual relationship between God and the Wisdom-Logos in eternity. The earthly life of Jesus has therefore disclosed the full mystery of what Jewish speculation had arrived at in its poetic personification of the Wisdom of God. Wisdom is now disclosed to be a personal entity within the Godhead existing in personal relationship with the being of the Father. This however is neither mythology nor speculation, but a revelation disclosed in the actual earthly life of Jesus. That which is incarnated in him (*ho logos sarx egeneto*, the Word became flesh) is a personal reality sharing the being of God yet distinguishable from him ("what God was, the Word was," NEB[17]). The disclosure of God in action in the man Jesus results in a profound modification of Jewish monotheism, but it is an enrichment of it, not its abandonment. The raw materials of the doctrine of the Trinity lie in the historical life of Jesus as the Fourth Evangelist had come to see it. If we are to be true to the profoundest understanding of the Jesus phenomenon, the preexistence and incarnation Christology cannot be abandoned. Rather, it is the foundation of the Christian understanding of God.

Notes

1. For a recent discussion of the Son of man problem, especially in its relation to preexistence Christology, see James D. G. Dunn, *Christology in the Making* (Philadelphia: Westminster Press, 1980), 65–97.

2. M. Hengel, "Christologie und neutestamentliche Chronologie," in *Neues Testament und Geschichte,* ed. H. Baltensweiler and B. Reicke (Tübingen: J. C. B. Mohr, 1972), 43–67.

3. See, e.g., J. Murphy-O'Connor, "Christological Anthropology in Phil. 2:6–11," *RB* 83 (1976): 25–50.

4. Hans Grass, *Christliche Glaubenslehre,* vol. 1 (2 vols.; Stuttgart: Kohlhammer, 1973–74), 117–38.

5. C. Colpe, *Die religionsgeschichtliche Schule* (Göttingen: Vandenhoeck & Ruprecht, 1961). It is ironic that my copy of this work was given to me personally by R. Bultmann, then editor of the series in which it was published, for it was the demolition of one of the foundations of his life's work.

6. See the discussion in Dunn, *Christology,* 98–101.

7. E. Schweizer, "Zur Herkunft der Präexistenzvorstellung bei Paulus," *EvT* 19 (1959): 65–70.

8. Dunn, *Christology,* 210.

9. A term coined by Edward Schillebeeckx, *Jesus* (New York: Seabury Press, 1979): 545–50.

10. E. Fuchs, *The Quest of the Historical Jesus* (London: SCM Press, 1964), 11–31, esp. pp. 20–21: "We are certainly confronted by a very daring line of conduct on the part of Jesus: he dares to affirm the will of God as though he himself stood in God's place."

11. Cf. Mark 12:1–9; Matt. 23:34–36 para Q.

12. The historical value of the kerygmatic speeches in Acts is much controverted. I take the mediating view of E. Schweizer, "Concerning the Speeches in Acts," in *Studies in Luke-Acts,* ed. Leander E. Keck and J. Louis Martyn (Nashville: Abingdon Press, 1966), 186–93, that the christological nucleus of these speeches is pre-Lucan and primitive. Luke's redaction interprets the earthly life of Jesus christologically, whereas the speeches interpret it in terms of a "theology of Jesus."

13. C. H. Dodd, in his Cambridge lectures on Pauline theology (1937), used this word to justify the development of preexistence Christology in Colossians.

14. Cf., e.g., Athanasius, *de Incarnatione.*

15. In the XXXIX Articles of Religion, articles I–VIII reaffirm the doctrine of the traditional Catholic creeds before continuing with the new soteriological emphases of the Reformation (Articles IX–XVIII).

16. I owe this phrase to my former colleague, Dr. Albert T. Mollegen, who used it in his Zabriskie Lectures of 1979.

17. The Greek text of John 1:1 reads *"theos"*—not *"ho theos"*—*"ēn ho logos."*

10

NEW TESTAMENT TRAJECTORIES
AND BIBLICAL AUTHORITY

The term *trajectory* was introduced into NT scholarship by J. M.
Robinson and Helmut Koester in their collection of essays published in the United States under the title *Trajectories Through Early
Christianity.*[1] Since this book has not been published in Britain, it
seems appropriate to spend some time indicating what is meant by
"trajectories."

The Robinson-Koester volume was also published in Germany, and the title of the German edition rendered "Trajectories"
as *Entwicklungslinien,* lines of development. This German rendition
explains in part what is meant by trajectories; but the latter word,
in addition to its contemporary flavor, is far more suggestive than
"lines of development." It is true that the word *trajectory* might suggest predetermined lines of development, but the two writers are
aware of this and deny any such intended suggestion in their use of
it: "The term trajectory may suggest too much determinative control at the initial point of departure, the angle at which the movement was launched, the torque of the initial thrust." The term is
not used in such a way as to suggest that the course of early Christian thought followed some theological or philosophically predetermined scheme, whether of predestination, apocalyptic denouement,
Hegelian dialectical process, prophecy fulfillment pattern, or the
like. Rather, it is meant to suggest that the future is open to all
possibilities of development. What then are the advantages of the

term? It suggests that the course of the history of NT thought is subject to conflicting fields of gravity, pulling it first this way, then that. It suggests that under these circumstances action may be taken to redirect that course, reversing it, twisting it, or modifying its speed. To keep up the metaphor, auxiliary guidance systems or retro-rockets can be employed.[2] Another possibility which has been opened up by the application of the trajectory principle to the history of early Christian thought is the possibility of bifurcation. A given trajectory may take two different courses, one leading to what later became orthodoxy and one (there could, of course, be more than one deviation) in the direction of what later came to be stigmatized by the Great Church as heresy. At this point the two authors acknowledged their dependence on W. Bauer's *Orthodoxy and Heresy in Earliest Christianity*.[3]

We have spoken of conflicting gravitational pulls, and this point needs further explication. Previous study of the beginnings of Christianity usually assigned study of the *Umwelt* or environment of earliest Christianity to NT Introduction. Once one had defined the various environmental factors—whether rabbinic Judaism, sectarian Judaism, the mystery religions, or gnosticism—these factors were conceived as static entities. But they are seen by Koester and Robinson as themselves passing through a trajectory of their own, which influenced the various Christian trajectories in different ways at different stages. The Christian trajectories must therefore always be studied in relation to the extra-Christian trajectories. We cannot treat non-Christian religious or cultural phenomena as static entities providing a fixed background for the development of early Christian thought.

It should be clear from the foregoing that despite the German rendering *Entwicklungslinien*, trajectories should not be thought of as straight-line developments, of the kind Newman posed in his classic essay. The Christian trajectories are subject to all the vicissitudes which are inescapable to the human situation of historicity.

The rest of the Robinson-Koester book is devoted to a study of a number of specific trajectories, some traced from one document to another, some from one generation to another. They involve both concepts (e.g., christological images) and different kinds of literary forms—called variously by the French term *genre* or the German *Gattung*.

The first study[4] takes up the modern categories of kerygma and history in the NT and shows that these are not static categories, but refer to trajectories which are constantly on the move. Under the term *kerygma* it examines how the pre-Pauline kerygmatic formulae became in Hellenistic Christianity a vehicle for an incipient gnostic understanding of Christian existence (1 Corinthians) and had to be corrected by Paul with a renewed emphasis upon the σταφοός, the cross of Christ, and upon the "not yet" of Paul's distinctive apocalyptic stance. The partial abandonment of this stance in the deutero-Pauline literature (Ephesians, Colossians) is then traced. On the side of history, the development of the interpretation of the historical Jesus as a θεῖος ἀνήο is studied, with particular reference to the correction of this Christology in Mark, Paul, and John.

Chapter three[5] traces the trajectory of the logia-*Gattung*—collections of Jesus' sayings. Starting with pre-Marcan collections, such as the source of the parable chapter (Mark 4) and the Q material, the fate of this *Gattung* is traced through its bifurcation into Matthew-Luke on the one hand, where it is combined with Mark and so integrated into the kerygma of the passion, and on the other hand into gnostic or semignostic collections such as the Nag Hammadi *Gospel of Thomas,* where the logia-*Gattung* is used to present the earthly Jesus as the purveyor of a gnostic-type heavenly wisdom. Chapter four[6] need not concern us as it is devoted to tracing the various types of Christianity in different local centers past the NT period, but Chapter five is perhaps the most important chapter in the book and very germane to our purpose, namely, an enquiry into the implications of the trajectory approach for the authority of the NT in the Christian church today. This chapter examines four different *Gattungen* in which the Jesus tradition crystallized: kerygmatic formulae, sayings collections, aretalogies, or collections of miracle stories and revelation discourses.[7] Again, the bifurcation of these *Gattungen* is stressed. On the one hand, when taken up by leading NT writers they are secured for what later developed into Christian orthodoxy. On the other hand, each of these *Gattungen,* allowed to drift off uncorrected on a course of its own, later becomes the potential vehicle for heretical presentations of Christianity.

Chapter six[8] deals with the various kerygmatic Christologies in the NT: Jesus as the apocalyptic Lord of the future, Jesus as Divine Man, Jesus as wisdom.

Chapter seven[9] studies the history of the Johannine tradition from the earliest units of Jesus material through the written miracle collection, then the evangelist's use of this material as a launching pad for his revelatory discourses, and finally the Johannine redactor's corrections of the evangelist, whose own corrections of the aretalogy with discourse material opened up the danger of further development in a gnostic direction (John's Gospel as a case almost of "out of the frying pan into the fire!").

The trajectory method as propounded by Robinson and Koester has provided a framework in which many other streams of Christian thought are being interpreted. Doctoral students are discovering further trajectories: professors are hitting upon new ones in their lectures. In particular, I would like to report on one use of the trajectory pattern in ecumenical dialogue. During the years 1971–73 a task force of NT scholars, Roman Catholic and Lutheran, an offshoot of the Lutheran-Catholic dialogue in the United States, has been studying the role of Peter in the New Testament. Two outsiders were co-opted, one Reformed and one Anglican, the latter of which I was privileged to be. We abandoned the simplistic use of Matt. 16:17–19 as conclusive evidence *pro* or *con* for the papacy and concentrated instead on how Peter was understood in the early Christian communities. We were interested less in the historical Simon and more in the ecclesiastical Cephas. Each relevant NT document was examined with all modern critical methods, including form-, tradition-, and redaction criticism. We assumed critical positions for the epistles and Acts, distinguishing the Pauline homologoumena and antilegomena, treating Acts as a product of the subapostolic age and, more important, as an expression of Lucan theology rather than as a history of the earliest community, and the church's epistles as pseudonymous writing of the subapostolic age.

Peter appeared to be quite central in early Christian thought.[10] We found ourselves reconstructing a trajectory of the images of Peter. In the period of the early Christian mission, Peter was portrayed as the great Christian fisherman (Mark 1:14–20; Luke 5:1–11; John 21:1–14). In the more settled situation of the subapostolic age, Peter is seen preeminently as the shepherd or pastor of the sheep (John 21:15–19; 1 Peter 5:1–4). In close connection with the image of the shepherd emerges the theme of Peter as the paradigm of martyrdom (John 13:7–8 following John 10:11, John 21:18–19; 1 Peter 5:1). Another part of the trajectory which became clear was that of Peter as the recipient of special revelation, originating no doubt from the tradition that he was the first to see the risen One (Mark 9:2ff.; 2 Peter 1:16–18; cf. also the revelatory experiences of Peter in Acts 5:1ff.; Acts 12:7–9). Directly related to this is the further picture of Peter as the confessor of the true Christian faith (Matt. 16:16–17; John 6:66–68). Out of this springs the final development in the NT trajectory of Peter, Peter as the guardian of faith against false teaching (2 Peter 1:20–21; 3:15–16). But all through the trajectory there is the picture of Peter as a weak and sinful human being. Permit me to quote our conclusion, for it is germane to our theme:

> Thus in early Christian thought, as attested by the New Testament, there is a plurality of images associated with Peter: missionary, fisherman, pastoral shepherd, martyr, recipient of special revelation, confessor of the true faith, magisterial protector and repentant sinner. When a trajectory of these images is traced, we find indications of development from earlier to later images.

We recognized that other trajectories can be traced in the NT—the trajectory of the Twelve or of Paul, for instance. But the Petrine trajectory eventually outdistanced the other apostolic trajectories. Thus in 2 Peter, Peter is invoked to correct the development of a Pauline trajectory in a gnostic direction. From this we went on to point out—and here is one of the distinctive advantages of the trajectory concept—that the trajectory does not end with the NT (the same awareness was shown in the Robinson–Koester volume, where the continuation of NT trajectories into post-NT orthodoxy and heresy was constantly recorded). This is what we say:

> Precisely because we have discovered the importance of the trajectory travelled by Peter's image, a trajectory that even in the New Testament is not coterminous with his historical career, this does not necessarily settle the question of Peter's importance for the subsequent church. The ecumenical discussion must involve not only the historical figure, but also the continuing trajectory of his image in the New Testament and beyond. To what extent is such a trajectory determined by the historical figure? To what extent is it determined by the accidents of history itself? [Here a footnote adds: Obviously there is another related question: To what extent has the later trajectory of Peter's image influenced the various Christian interpretations of Peter's roles in the New Testament? In short, the question of the effect of theological retrojection upon exegesis.] And whatever way we answer these questions, how does God's providence and His will for His church enter into the trajectory?

I quote this passage at length because it asks some of the systematic questions raised by the trajectory method, questions with which the remainder of this chapter will be concerned. On the one hand there are clear gains for theology and exegesis from the trajectory approach. First, it has reinforced the effect of form criticism in loosening up the older rigid distinction between scripture and tradition. Form criticism had shown that the Gospels were themselves the depository of tradition, while the work of A. Seeberg, E. Meyer and later of P. Carrington and E. G. Selwyn showed that this was also true of the epistles, which likewise enshrine many traditional formulae—kerygmatic, credal, liturgical, and catechetical. The trajectory method has dealt another blow to this rigid distinction between scripture and tradition, for the NT is now seen as evidence for movements of thought which continue on their way into the period after the canon. The NT writings break off when the trajectories are still in midcourse. For instance, we do not find the papacy in the Petrine texts, but we do find a trajectory which, for good or ill, was destined to produce one particular climax in the decrees of Vatican I. Scripture is now rightly seen as part of the ongoing tradition of Christian faith and life. The trajectory method has likewise reinforced the pluralistic view of the NT. C. H. Dodd sought to discover a single kerygma which underlay all the writings of the NT.[11] But he achieved this by combining in an artificial synthesis a number of different kerygmatic formulae. E. Käsemann has shown that the NT exhibits rather a plurality of kerygmata,[12] thus leading to a search for a canon behind the canon.[13] The trajectory method has reinforced this awareness of the pluralism, and indeed extended it. It is no longer simply a matter of a plurality of kerygmata existing side by side, so that the question is merely, Which kerygma? The kerygmata themselves are now seen to be involved in a process of change and development, so that the question now becomes, Which kerygma at what stage of its development, at what point in its trajectory? The NT is not a single static document, universally applicable as a norm of proclamation and doctrine, but a record of many different trajectories at many different stages of development. How then is it possible to apply such a canon as a norm? If there is no such thing as orthodoxy in the NT, and if orthodoxy, as Koester and Robinson following W. Bauer assert, emerged later, what is the point of looking for an orthodox norm so early as the NT documents? Is not the only solution to follow the method of J. Wren-Lewis as cited by John A. T. Robinson:[14] "All we can say is 'I believe in the values of the Roman Catholic Church,' or 'the Evangelical Christian tradition,' or 'British Public School Christianity.'" Or, to put it in another way, should we not follow B. H. Streeter's verdict on the relative justification of different forms of church polity with the *Alice in Wonderland* verdict that "Everyone has won, and all shall have prizes."[15] The trajectory method, helpful as it is for the understanding of the historical processes of the development of early Christian thought, seems to reduce all Christian truth to a pluralistic relativism.

Added to this is the further problem of hermeneutics, so well illustrated in Robinson-Koester, the problem that by repeating the same thing in a changed situation you end up by saying precisely the opposite. A statement which is orthodox in one situation can be heretical in another. Nowhere is this more clearly shown than by the difference between the line taken by Paul in First Corinthians, and that which he takes in Second. Against the local gnosticizers[16] in Corinth Paul insists that one must hold at all costs to the sarkic Jesus. No one can say Ἰησοῦς ἀνάθεμα ("To hell with the historical Jesus," 1 Cor. 12:3) if he speaks through the Holy Spirit. The Christian gnostics regarded the historical life of Jesus as a temporary episode in the ongoing revelation of wisdom. What mattered now was that as the risen One he communicates still, as he did on earth, the heavenly wisdom to the initiated. In 2 Corinthians, on the other hand, Paul is confronted with a very different situation. Wandering preachers claimed themselves to be θεῖοι ἄνδοες in direct continuity with the historical Jesus (thus they preached "another Jesus," 2 Cor. 11:4). Against this Paul has to repudiate any adherence to *Christos* known κατὰ σάοκα (2 Cor. 5:16), and insists on knowing Χοιστὸς κατὰ πνεῦμα, the very thing he rejected so strongly in 1 Corinthians. So even if we could locate one Archimedian point in the total NT witness and make that the permanent criterion for Christian proclamation, faith, and life, that would be of no avail. For that point, reasserted in a new situation, could have precisely the opposite effect.

Now Helmut Koester is not oblivious of this need for a criterion or norm by which to assess the various kerygmata of the NT, and the church's continuing proclamation today. He first cites Ernst Käsemann's question,[17] "Does the New Testament kerygma count the historical Jesus among the criteria of its own validity?" and goes on to make the following proposal:

> Accordingly we are confronted not with the quest for a new image of Jesus to be used as the norm for true belief, but with the question, whether and in which [sic: a Germanism] way that which has happened historically, i.e., in the earthly Jesus of Nazareth, is present in each given case as

the criterion—not necessarily the content—of Christian proclamation and theology. Only in this way can our inquiry arrive at an evaluation of the orthodox and heretical tendencies of each new historical situation—certainly not in order to open a new heresy trial over the early Christian literature, but in order to recognize in which [again sic] way the criterion for true Christian faith, consciously or unconsciously, structured the reinterpretation of the religious traditions and presuppositions upon which Christianity was dependent.

This is a highly important statement and calls for detailed comment. First, we note that it appears to take a somewhat different line from Robinson, who, as we have seen, questioned whether the term *trajectory* might suggest too much determinative control at the initial point of departure.[18] But perhaps the two statements might be reconciled if the modifier "determinative" is stressed in Robinson's statement. It is obviously not a case of automatic, inevitable determination, but of a criterion which has to be fought for and applied delicately in each successive situation, as the example of Paul in First and Second Corinthians shows. A second point to be observed is that Koester is taking up one particular side in the so-called new quest of the historical Jesus, namely, the side of the new questers against the kerygmatists.[19] In my review of Robinson's book *A New Quest of the Historical Jesus,* I opted firmly for the position of the kerygmatists against that of the new questers.[20] In other words, I opted for the kerygma of the post-Easter church rather than for the historical Jesus as the norm of Christian proclamation and faith. The reason for this was that in my view the historical Jesus was made out of date by Easter, since the eschatological purpose of God had advanced further by Easter itself. Today I would not speak of the historical Jesus' being made out of date, for that has since been exposed as precisely the position of the Corinthian gnostics. But I still think that Easter must be taken up into the norm, or, if you will, the norm of the historical Jesus must be the historical Jesus as seen through the perspective of Easter faith. Koester's norm, if it stood by itself without qualification might lead, contrary I am sure to his intention, to an acceptance of the legitimacy of the ἄλλος Ἰησοῦς of the wandering preachers in Second Corinthians. After all, the historical Jesus did perform exorcisms! Yet a one-sided preference for the kerygma is equally fraught with danger, as First Corinthians shows. The Corinthian gnosticizers accepted the exalted Lord as the continuing purveyor of wisdom, but relegated the historical Jesus to the archives. Moreover, as we have already seen, modern scholarship has demonstrated the plurality of the kerygmata, and that inevitably raises the question, Which kerygma?

If we are to find the answer to our search for an Archimedian point, it would be well to take another look at the way in which the Jesus traditions were finally absorbed into the documents of the New Testament. We begin with the Pauline homologoumena, Mark, Matthew-Luke, and John. Luke-Acts, the deutero-Pauline literature, and the other later NT writings pose special problems which require separate treatment.

Paul, as J. M. Robinson has shown, has taken up the wisdom Christology of the Corinthians, akin, he thinks, to the Christology of the Q tradition, and has corrected it with the insistence that the focal point of the wisdom Christology manifested in Jesus is not to be found in the sayings of Jesus per se, but in his death upon the cross which the sayings interpret. This event inaugurates a salvific process which will not be completed until the *parousia* (1 Cor. 1–4; 15). The corrective principle which Paul applies to Corinthian wisdom-gnosis is the kerygma of the cross, prefaced by the wisdom material in the earthly Jesus tradition, and followed by the proclamation of his resurrection seen in the context of the still outstanding *parousia*. His corrective principle is thus not the bare fact of the cross, but the cross set in a context of before and after. Paul's procedure is a carefully nuanced one, and it would be easy, as it was easy for the Valentinians in the second century,[21] to isolate one aspect of it—in their case the wisdom aspect of the kerygma—and to interpret Paul in a completely gnostic sense. One can easily understand how they managed this by reading 1 Corinthians 2:6–16 out of context with the rest of the epistle with the latter's insistence on the centrality of the cross and the apocalyptic "not yet." What matters is the corrective principle that Paul applies. The same is true, though almost in the opposite direction, of Second Corinthians. Here, as Georgi has shown, an aretalogical Jesus tradition has been corrected by a cross-centered kerygma. It is not in the aretalogical tradition that shines through Second Corinthians, but in the corrective principle applied, that the nub of the Pauline message is to be found.

Similarly, the heart of the Marcan message is to be found in the corrective which he applied to his aretalogical sources.[22] This he achieved by using the aretalogies as a preface for a passion narrative by the device of the messianic secret, and by the body of teaching enshrined in the section 8:27–10:45.[23] In this way, the pre-Marcan miracle stories become prefigurations (to use Austin Farrer's term) of the ultimate messianic miracle which is the cross.

John, too, follows an analogous procedure, though in his own way. He utilizes a more highly aretalogical tradition[24] than Mark had, uses it as a launching pad for revelation discourses and dialogues and, like Mark,[25] makes this composite material a prelude to the passion narrative. The passion is thus interpreted as the ultimate manifestation of the divine glory prefigured in the words and works of the historical Jesus. But just as Paul had laid himself open to a gnostic (Valentinian) interpretation in 1 Cor. 2:6–16, so John exposed himself to misinterpretation by some of his unguarded statements about Christology[26] and the degree of realization in Jesus' offer of eternal life through his word. Therefore his work probably had to be corrected again by a redactor from within the Johannine school.[27] As we have already noted, the Johannine trajectory received a correction from the evangelist which went a little too far in the other direction, and had itself to be corrected with a renewed emphasis on the "not yet" and on the flesh and blood as well as the bread from heaven.

It would seem that we are now in principle able to find what we are looking for. The Archimedian point, the basic norm for Christian proclamation, a faith and life, is to be found not in the NT writings as such, but in the correctives they apply to the ongoing Christian trajectories. This correction in each instance involves the earthly Jesus who was crucified and whose redemptive deed in the crucifixion is perpetuated in the exaltation and consummated in the *parousia*. The corrective seems to be the one stable element, though applied differently in each specific instance since something different has to be corrected. The NT provides us therefore not only with the initial impulse of Christian trajectories, but also with the corrective principles which have constantly to be applied anew as Christian thought develops.

But what of the double work of Luke and the post-Pauline epistolary literature? Do these exhibit the same corrective principles?

Luke-Acts appears to contain far too much uncorrected aretalogical material. Take, for instance, Luke's treatment of Jesus at prayer. Whereas Mark and special source of Luke present Jesus' prayer as arising out of crisis situations, it is characteristic of Luke's redaction that Jesus prays in order to replenish his δύναμις of which he had been drained in the performance of his miracles. Acts is even more strongly aretalogical. On listening to the NEB version of Paul's contest with the μάγος Elymas in Acts 13:4–12 a little while ago I was shocked how Paul was represented simply as a competing μάγος who happened to be more successful, and I wondered what the historical Paul of 2 Corinthians 10–13 would have made of it. Luke-Acts contains much raw, uncorrected θεῖος ἀνήο material as embarrassing to the contemporary NT scholar as it is to the educated layman. Can it be part of the norm? Are we to say that Luke is to be accepted not for his redaction, as was the case with the other main NT writings, but only for some of the traditions he preserves (the Q material safely embedded as in Matthew, in the Marcan Gospel form and the early kerygmatic material in the speeches of Acts)? Fortunately, there is another side to Luke, and this is his setting of the Christ event and the ongoing life of the Christian community in a framework of salvation history. I know that this has been castigated by the Bultmann school as an early catholicizing of the Pauline-Marcan eschatological message, but it should be understood as precisely a correction of a gnosticizing trajectory in the subapostolic age.[28] In this framework the embarrassing aretalogical materials are, I suggest, neutralized and rendered innocuous, for they are made subservient to the purpose of God in salvation history. Within this framework, too, the cross has its place, despite the recent castigation of Luke for this lack of a theology of the cross. For the cross is comprehended under the apocalyptic δεῖ, [29] a divine necessity in the working out of God's purpose in *Heilsgeschichte*. This lacks the profundity, no doubt, of the soteriological interpretations of the cross in the pre-Pauline formulae and in the Pauline theology of justification. But it cannot be said that Luke-Acts lacks a *theologia crucis* altogether. If the longer text of the Supper narrative is accepted in accordance with current trends (Luke 22:19b–20), then Luke even has a ὑπέο theology of the atonement.

Finally, there are the deutero-Pauline writings and the other post-Pauline epistolary literature. Can these be regarded as part of the norm? Or are these writings representative of uncorrected trajectories? In the main and in various degrees, Colossians, Ephesians, the Pastorals, Hebrews, and 1 Peter preserve the Pauline heritage in the subapostolic age and adjust it to new conditions. Thus they may be accepted with little question as a legitimate continuation of the Pauline trajectory. Similarly, the Johannine epistles may be regarded as a continuation of the Johannine trajectory, probably along the lines set by the redactor of the Fourth Gospel (1 John may even have been the redactor's work). The real problem concerns the legitimacy of early Catholicism as such, elements of which are found to be present in varying degrees in most of the post-Pauline writings, and in its most virulent form in 2 Peter. Is the early catholic trajectory a misdirected one? It could be argued that the early catholic developments—an institutionalized ministry, creed, liturgy, catechesis, developing magisterium, and so forth—were not only necessary in that age in order to preserve the earlier NT trajectories on course, but provide a permanently valid paradigm for their preservation today. And by preserving the Pauline homologoumena and the Gospels, the early catholic writings of the NT preserved also their own corrective.

We are now, I think, in the position to answer some of the questions which this chapter posed at the outset. Given the pluralism of the NT; given the fact that early Christian thought is constantly on the move; given, too, the fact that no position can be definitive because of the basic hermeneutical problem that a position asserted in one situation can mean something very different, perhaps even the precise opposite of its original meaning when repeated in a new situation; given in short all the problems about the authority of the NT which arise from the concept of trajectories; in what sense can the NT be normative for the proclamation, faith, and life of the Christian community today? The answer lies, I suggest, in the *directionality* given to the trajectories by the great NT writers, Paul, Mark, John, and the other NT writings consonant therewith. Broadly speaking, the NT provides direction for its trajectories, a directionality which is applied by the main NT writers to trajectories when they are threatening to deviate from the course initiated by the Christ event. The question that always has to be asked of contemporary Christian proclamation, faith, and life is not whether they correctly reproduce NT Christianity, or even one particular phase of NT Christianity, such as Paul, Mark, or John, but rather, do they maintain that course, that directionality, in the totally different historical situation today?

Finally, we may now approach that question asked by the task force on Peter, namely, whether God's providence and his will for his church enter into the trajectory. Robinson and Koester were right when they eschewed the suggestion that a positive answer to this question should be assumed as an a priori to their enterprise in tracing early Christian trajectories. Such an answer can only come as a confession of faith at the end of an analysis, never as its presupposition. But for all their pluralism and variety, we have found a remarkable consistency of direction between the principal writers of the NT. I am not even sure whether Bauer was entirely right in defining orthodoxy as a type of Christianity which finally emerged only in the second century out of the pluralistic possibilities of the first century-and-a-half in the history of Christian thought. If we view orthodoxy not as a static datum, but as a direction, then we may see an orthodox direction present in a trajectory which runs from the Christ event through the earliest kerygma, the three main NT authors, the apologists, the church fathers (some of them, no doubt, not all), and the Reformation confessions.

The discovery of early Christian trajectories should increase our confidence in the processes by which the canon of the NT finally came into being. In this corpus, the dominant place is occupied by the Pauline homologoumena and the four Gospels—precisely those writings where (with the partial exception of Luke) the corrective to dangerously developing trajectories is most apparent. There is no reason, in the light of the early Christian trajectories, why the church should not confess that it is these particular writings that are authoritative norms for her continuing proclamation, faith, and life, and that it is the providence of God and his Holy Spirit that can be seen by faith, after the event, at work in and through this very human process, the formation of the NT canon.

Notes

1. J. M. Robinson and Helmut Koestler, *Trajectories Through Early Christianity* (Philadelphia: Fortress Press, 1971). The SCM Press was offered the British rights on this book, but turned them down on the grounds that it did not appear "all that interesting" (Letter of the editor, J. Bowden, to R. H. Fuller, dated January 29, 1973). He promised to reconsider publication if the rights were still free.

2. Ibid., 14.

3. W. Bauer, *Orthodoxy and Heresy in Earliest Christianity* (Philadelphia: Fortress Press, 1971); ET of *Rechtgläubigkeit und Ketzerei im ältesten Christentum* (²1964).

4. Robinson, "Kerygma and History in the New Testament," in *Trajectories*, 20–70.

5. Ibid., "Logoi Sophon: On the Gattung of Q," in *Trajectories*, 71–113.

6. Koester, "Gnomai Diaphorai: The Origin and Nature of Diversification in the History of Early Christianity," in *Trajectories*, 114–57.

7. Ibid., "One Jesus and Four Primitive Gospels," in *Trajectories*, 158–204.

8. Ibid., "The Structure and Criteria of Early Christian Beliefs," in *Trajectories*, 205–31.

9. Robinson, "The Johannine Trajectory," in *Trajectories*, 232–68.

10. R. E. Brown et al., *Peter in the New Testament* (New York: Paulist Press; Minneapolis: Augsburg Publishing House, 1973).

11. C. H. Dodd, *The Apostolic Preaching and Its Developments* (London: Hodder & Stoughton, ¹1936). See the summary on p. 17 of the 1949 ed.

12. E. Käsemann, *Essays on New Testament Themes* (London: SCM Press, 1964), speaks of the "variability of the primitive Christian kerygma" (p. 100; cf. p. 103).

13. Käsemann, *Essays*, 57f., who finds the canon within the canon in the NT message of the justification of the sinner.

14. John A. T. Robinson, *The Human Face of God* (London: SCM Press, 1973), 30.

15. B. H. Streeter, *The Primitive Church* (London: Macmillan & Co., 1930), viii.

16. 1 Cor. 12:3 has been interpreted in many different ways. The interpretation given in the text was first proposed by W. Schmithals, *Gnosticism in Corinth* (Nashville/New York: Abingdon Press, 1971), 126. It is followed by J. M. Robinson, *Trajectories*, 22.

17. Koester, *Trajectories*, 160 and n. 7.

18. Ibid., 14.

19. For the distinction between the "new questers" and the "kerygmatists," see R. H. Fuller, *The New Testament in Current Study* (New York: Charles Scribner's Sons, 1961), 25–52. The "new questers," notably Fuchs, Ebeling, Braun, and J. M. Robinson himself, regard the historical Jesus as an alternative focus for Christian faith in lieu of the kerygma, and the kerygma as a vehicle for repristinating the historical Jesus. The "kerygmatists" (Käsemann, Conzelmann, Bornkamm, Hahn) regard the new quest as a legitimate enterprise for establishing the continuity between Jesus and the kerygma, but continue to maintain that the kerygma is the focus of Christian faith.

20. *ATR* 41 (1959): 232–35.

21. Elaine H. Pagels has assembled examples of Valentinian exegesis of Paul in *The Gnostic Paul: Gnostic Exegesis of the Pauline Letters* (Philadelphia: Fortress Press, 1975). Cf. her similar study of gnostic exegesis of John, *The Johannine Gospel in Gnostic Exegesis*, SBL Monograph 17 (Nashville/New York: Abingdon Press, 1973).

22. For Mark's aretalogical sources, cf. P. Achtemeier, "Toward the Isolation of Pre-Marcan Catenae," *JBL* 89 (1970): 265–91; and idem, "The Origin and Function of the pre-Marcan Catenae," *JBL* 91

(1972): 198–221. For the Marcan corrective, cf. T. J. Weeden, *Mark—Traditions in Conflict* (Philadelphia: Fortress Press, 1971) and N. Perrin in *Christology: A Modern Pilgrimage,* ed. H. Betz (Philadelphia: Fortress Press, 1974), 1–78. One may agree that Mark has provided a corrective to a *theios anēr* Christology without accepting these authors' particular views about Mark's treatment of the disciples.

23. See Perrin's structural analysis of Mark in his essay cited above, n. 22.

24. For John's aretalogical source, see R. Bultmann, *The Gospel of John* (Philadelphia: Westminster Press, 1971); W. Wilckens, *Zeichen und Werke* (Zürich: Zwingli Verlag, 1969); J. Becker, "Wunder und Christologie," *NTS* 16 (1970): 130–48; R. T. Fortna, "Source and Redaction in the Fourth Gospel's Portrayal of Jesus' Signs," *JBL* 89 (1970): 151–66.

25. I find unconvincing R. T. Fortna's thesis that John's narrative source was a gospel in which the passion narrative was already prefixed with miracles. See R. T. Fortna, *The Signs Gospel* (London: Cambridge University Press, 1970).

26. Jesus appears in John 6 as the Bread from Heaven, a Christology susceptible of a gnostic interpretation with Jesus as the bearer of heavenly gnosis. The redactor sought to avert this peril by the addition of John 6:51–58.

27. Thus R. E. Brown's modification of Bultmann's ecclesiastical redactor hypothesis. See R. E. Brown, *The Gospel According to John* (Garden City, N.Y.: Doubleday & Co., 1966), xxxix.

28. For an antignostic *Sitz im Leben* for Luke-Acts, see C. H. Talbert, *Luke and the Gnostics* (Nashville: Abingdon Press, 1966).

29. E. Fascher, "Theologische Beobachtungen zu δεῖ," in *Neutestamentliche Studien für R. Bultmann,* ed. W. Eltester (Berlin: Töpelmann, 1954), 228–54.

INDEX OF
BIBLICAL REFERENCES